Dear Terry
With Best wishes
Miti

THE
INNOVATIVE
COMMUNICATOR

Putting the soul back into business communication

Miti Ampoma

BALBOA.
PRESS
A DIVISION OF HAY HOUSE

Copyright © 2012 Miti Ampoma
Cover Design – © ByDeesign
Author's photo – © John Cassidy Headshots

All rights reserved. No part of this book may be used or reproduced by any means, graphic, electronic, or mechanical, including photocopying, recording, taping or by any information storage retrieval system without the written permission of the publisher except in the case of brief quotations embodied in critical articles and reviews.

Balboa Press books may be ordered through booksellers or by contacting:

Balboa Press
A Division of Hay House
1663 Liberty Drive
Bloomington, IN 47403
www.balboapress.com
1-(877) 407-4847

ISBN: 978-1-4525-5684-0 (sc)
ISBN: 978-1-4525-5685-7 (hc)
ISBN: 978-1-4525-5683-3 (e)

Library of Congress Control Number: 2012914711

Because of the dynamic nature of the Internet, any web addresses or links contained in this book may have changed since publication and may no longer be valid. The views expressed in this work are solely those of the author and do not necessarily reflect the views of the publisher, and the publisher hereby disclaims any responsibility for them.

The author of this book does not dispense medical advice or prescribe the use of any technique as a form of treatment for physical, emotional, or medical problems without the advice of a physician, either directly or indirectly. The intent of the author is only to offer information of a general nature to help you in your quest for emotional and spiritual well-being. In the event you use any of the information in this book for yourself, which is your constitutional right, the author and the publisher assume no responsibility for your actions.

Any people depicted in stock imagery provided by Thinkstock are models, and such images are being used for illustrative purposes only.
Certain stock imagery © Thinkstock.

Printed in the United States of America

Balboa Press rev. date: 09/21/2012

Dedication

I dedicate this book to Sarah Moon, Sue Turner, Monica Jönsson-Rayel and Paulette Brooks, each a life changing Innovative Communicator in their professional field of expertise. From you I have learnt so much. Thank you.

My profuse thanks

My profuse thanks and a big hug to my writing coach and book editor Judy Dendy, without whom this book would not have happened. I knew I had a great editor when she quoted my chapter title at me during a tough writing patch "Well Miti, it's all about pushing your own boundaries!" ☺

Table of Contents

Introduction ix

Chapter 1
Meet the Innovative Communicator 1

Chapter 2
Build deep relationships 16

Chapter 3
Get your team on board 46

Chapter 4
Build your strategy 67

Chapter 5
Push your own boundaries 100

Chapter 6
Step forward with courage 111

Chapter 7
Get tough with heart 125

Chapter 8
Have a life to bring to the table 153

Chapter 9
Keep sparkling 162

Introduction

> *"The soul has been stripped out of the way the business world communicates and it desperately needs putting back. Powerful communication between people plays a critical role in a company's bottom line. It is not a "soft" skill, a nice to have or a fluffy optional extra. Without it, you're toast!"*
> **Miti Ampoma**

In April 2012, over the Easter holidays, a national newspaper reported that a well-known large business, a household name, "apologised to thousands of customers after confidential information about their finances was sent to the wrong people. The blunder by the company had led to customers receiving details of other people's pension plans which revealed personal sensitive data. The mistake raised serious questions about data protection, particularly as the information could be of use to identify thieves."

The letter of apology, the company's form of communication, signed by the organisation's "Customer Experience Director" was instructive. In his apology he said, "Please be assured that [we] take all errors of this nature seriously and have put in place actions necessary to prevent it from happening again and to ensure the safeguarding of your policy information." But this is the bit that really struck me. Worried customers seeking more information about the blunder were given the number of a helpline BUT the letter added, "There will be no one taking calls over the Easter holiday."!

To me, this is a classic communication, public relations disaster. A classic big business with no soul. It is not just poor customer service. At the heart of this, is a level of impersonality which amounts to crass communication. From the unhappy customers' point of view, there is a serious likelihood that the Data Protection Act designed to protect them may have been breached, their personal information has gone to someone else, they've been asked to destroy the sensitive data that they've received that isn't their own, they've been given warm meaningless words in a letter about caring and yet the action and behaviour to back up those words is the opposite. The bottom line is there is actually no one they can contact to talk to about the blunder for four days, because the blunder happens to fall over the Easter holiday weekend and no provision has been made for this, despite these extenuating circumstances! Surely for the majority of people, this must read as a poor way forward.

I believe the soul has been stripped out of the way the business world communicates and it desperately needs putting back. I want to put it back.

At the heart of most businesses there are **people, process and technology.** Prior to advanced technology, people were naturally the heart of a business. This focus made them the priority. As modern businesses developed, strong processes were required to enable operational discipline and efficiency. Processes (deliberately or otherwise) crept ahead of people as the priority, so we got **process, people, technology.** The revolutionary impact of technology on businesses has changed priorities further. It is fair to say that for many large businesses, for a variety of reasons, the order of priority has moved to **technology, process, people.**

Could this be you? You're a big business or a complex one. You might also be growing and employing more people. You've got more than 2000 employees. You don't quite know when it began, but somehow your people seem disconnected with the business, disengaged and disaffected. They work or seem to, but aren't really *feeling* your goals. It's uphill. Strong, effective motivating communication between people in your business isn't happening as it should. It all feels stuck despite the communication, the Human Resources (HR) team and the external hired help in place – somehow the heart and the soul of your business is evaporating. All this hurts because it's impacting your bottom line – and in a fiercely competitive commercial world you can't afford that. What can you do?

For the past fifteen years, I've worked with large organisations, FTSE 100 companies, financial services and corporate institutions, helping them to communicate more effectively with their staff and customers. During that time I've created and delivered tailor-made people-to-people communication programmes that have consistently sorted out people-chaos, and resulted in happy staff, happy customers and more profits. This has been achieved in good times as well as in times of crisis or huge change.

The key to every successful communication strategy has been putting the "heart and soul" back into the business, something many large organisations find increasingly difficult and challenging to do. This book is about how you as a leader can make that happen.

It's fundamentally about people. It's about getting lots of people in your business buzzed and inspired once more through the power of effective communication, to get them on side to be part of your business solutions – whatever the business weather.

My mission is to change the way the business world communicates. A business that places a genuine focus on integrity and humanity at the heart of its communication strategy will reap the benefits in three major ways:

- They will see communication between people drive performance
- Profits will increase and be sustainable
- The business will create a more positive impact in the world

I wrote this book for leaders in large or complex organisations but it is not another leadership book. Leadership, like Customer Service or Human Resources (HR) is one of many business components that have communication as their fundamental common denominator. These components are part of a critical junction box driven by the quality of your communication and ability to re-connect your people with each other. Mastering the art of communication is how you get the heart of your business back, stay in top shape and be the business you want to stand for. So, this book is for three levels of leaders in business:

- CEOs, top level directors and executives
- Managers who manage teams

- Team Leaders who are responsible for front line staff

As businesses get bigger or more complex, I've consistently found that the more people you've got, the higher the likelihood you'll have communication problems that impact your bottom line.

> ***Your people are dealing with lots of change, pressure to perform, business goals and targets they need to understand and meet . . . and the mistake is that you assume they understand what you want. That's not what happens.***

Instead, there are unnecessary delays and highly expensive recurring mistakes that just don't seem to resolve. Problems typically show up as unhappy customers and disgruntled employees with their arms folded, rumour mills, corridor conversations and no buy-in. So ultimately, the proof is that the required performance just isn't there. And the bigger your organisation, the more likelihood of these problems.

You want your people to understand your goals and work as a team to provide solutions. To do this you need:

- Clear, bold, effective communication with eyeball-to-eyeball contact between people to drive performance

- A people-centred strategy for communicating key messages (sometimes grim news) with integrity, respect and heart

In a tough business climate we need to communicate boldly and differently

I have created and introduce to you, the Innovative Communicator. The Innovative Communicator puts people at the heart of their business.

The Innovative Communicator is not someone you employ, or a role or function you leave to your HR or communication department. The Innovative Communicator is about someone you yourself can become, it's about qualities you can develop in yourself and in so doing, encourage others to do the same. It sets you up firmly as a communication role model in your business. It is more than just leadership training as you will discover when you read this book.

The Innovative Communicator knows how to build relationships, and how to get the team on board. The Innovative Communicator thinks outside the box, pushes their own boundaries and steps forward with courage. The Innovative Communicator is approachable, honest and warm, has a life to bring to the table and knows how to get tough with heart.

In fact, the Innovative Communicator's technique is based on good solid common sense, and while many readers will recognise this, the norm has proved increasingly challenging to achieve in large-scale businesses. This book is about what to do to make that happen.

The proven benefits of being an Innovative Communicator are:

- Your teams, your people and your business radiate with genuine engagement and good will. They feel valued and understood and will stick with you through thick and thin.

- Your people adopt the qualities of the Innovative Communicator that you yourself role model. It enables innovation to thrive.

- The left hand knows what the right hand is doing because communication between people becomes part of the DNA of the business.

- Energy is concentrated on growing your business profitably and ensuring it thrives because people genuinely feel "we are in this together".

In this book I've included many case studies from my own experience. Each one is real – with names and places changed to protect identities and respect confidentiality. Every person in the book is someone I have met, worked with, and in many cases come to know well. The scenarios and stories are taken from business programmes and projects for which I was responsible. However, as you read them, don't try to be me – draw from each one whatever interests you and applies to your business.

- You are aiming to develop some or all of the qualities and skills. Read through the book and pick out what you can start to apply. Perhaps you are doing it already (great!) or perhaps you can push your boundaries and try something challenging.

- Everyone learns in different ways. For logical learners there is bulleted information, summaries and questions, for experiential learners there are dialogues and case studies. I hope you will enjoy all of them.

- Pull out the generic principles and do it for yourself.

- Many of the principles and applications in this book can be applied to other areas of life. They are not rocket science. They are rooted in common sense.

- You may not agree with everything in this book, but I do wish and hope its content pushes your boundaries of thinking.

Above all, I want you to take the following key messages to heart – these are my Golden Rules:

- Great communication means great business these days. Bad communication is bad business all days!

- Good communication is no longer a soft skill, a nice to have or a fluffy optional extra tagged at the end of major business decisions.

- It is no longer good enough just to leave communication between your people to your HR, communication department or experts. In a new business climate you need to become a savvy communicator too.

- The way in which you (and your teams) communicate will enable your people to feel valued and understood, despite tricky times and difficult circumstances.

- People need to trust and believe what you say.

- Trust and integrity require demonstrable action in personal behaviour and communication.

How you achieve these golden rules is the key to your success.
Welcome to the Innovative Communicator!

1

Meet the Innovative Communicator

> *"There has never been a better time for people in business to reconnect through meaningful communication, to what matters most to them and to each other, for the greater good."*
> **Miti Ampoma**

Miranda – Flower-stall business owner

Miranda is a real person – I buy my flowers from her – and this is her story. She is a business owner, a business manager and a team leader, as she employs staff. She may not be a Chief Executive Officer (CEO) in a FTSE 100 company, but the way she runs her business beautifully illustrates what I see as the Innovative Communicator and here's why:

Miranda runs a flower stall in the middle of a busy local high street. Her stall is surrounded by three large national supermarkets that also sell flowers, some the same as Miranda's, at a cheaper price.

Since the economic down-turn, the other three independent flower-stall business owners in this high street have gone bust.

In fact, Miranda is the only independent flower-stall owner left in the high street. With four years of the toughest economic conditions known in recent times, Miranda's flower stall has not only survived, but thrives amid the business chaos and intense competition around her. Why?

The Innovative Communicator

For almost four years, I've watched with curiosity and fascination at the way Miranda operates her business. I have talked to her customers to find out and understand what they like about Miranda and their feedback has been consistent.

Firstly, Miranda is extremely personable. People warm to her. She makes every customer feel important and gives them her full attention, no matter how busy she is. She has trained her assistants to do the same.

Customers genuinely feel Miranda cares about them and wants to ensure that they leave her and her flower stall with the best flowers for them.

Secondly, Miranda knows her flowers inside out. She is an expert at her trade. She gets up at the crack of dawn and goes to the flower market herself. She is instrumental in making choices about which flowers end up on her stalls for sale to her customers. When she or her team are asked for advice on what flowers are best for an occasion, or to suggest a winning combination for a loved one, Miranda and her team's advice is professional, caring, personal, bespoke and spot on, delighting her customers. This is the huge emotional benefit for the buyer of Miranda's flowers.

Thirdly, Miranda's flowers are beautiful and fresh and according to her customers, last a lot longer than the cheaper supermarket flowers. Above all, Miranda makes her customers feel they are part of a local community.

Miranda has built deep long-lasting relationships with her customers. In return she has banked their unreserved trust and loyalty.

Miranda's customers adore her for who she is, for the emotional benefits and experience she gives them through her business, for her supreme customer service and for her superb style, range and quality of flowers.

For these reasons, customers in this high street are very happy to spend that extra money on Miranda's flowers. A typical Miranda customer will first do their shopping, often in the supermarket next door, buy everything they need except for flowers, and then go and buy the same flowers (they could have bought more cheaply in the supermarket, but chose not to) at Miranda's. On any typical busy Saturday morning in the high street Miranda's flowers will be sold out by early afternoon. Due to popularity, customers will often pop round and say "Save those tulips for me will you? I'll pop by and get them after shopping." Miranda will put those flowers aside and the customer will turn up and that is when they pay for it. The trust between Miranda and her customers to do the right thing for each other is notable.

The single common feature in all the attributes consistently described to me about Miranda, by both her customers as well her team, is the way in which she treats them through her daily interaction and communication. She is smart, highly gifted, admired and gracious in her strengths. She is also genuine, open-hearted and radiates integrity. People want to be around her and to actively support her business to flourish. Her flower business continues to go from strength to strength, regardless of the turbulent business environment.

David – CEO of a multi-million pound company

David is also an Innovative Communicator, and here is his story:

David is the CEO of a multi-million pound business, which includes a brokerage firm and a hugely successful IT division. He has hundreds of employees. He is an extremely busy man. He is known and respected in his industry as a tough, astute businessman. At a time, when the economic climate is producing continuous headlines of plunging profits, business closures of once iconic institutions and the bankruptcy of competitors, David's large business, amid the gloomy pandemonium, is reporting rising profits. He is employing more staff, and his existing employees stay put not out of dissatisfaction, but out of a fierce loyalty and genuine affection for him.

Many of David's staff have worked under his leadership for several years. David's business is bucking the economic trend. I was given permission to talk to David's employees, because like Miranda's flower business, I was curious and fascinated to understand why David's business is doing well in a dire economic climate, while many of his competitors are not. In my research when talking to the company's employees, there was one particular story which stood out and summed up the source of the organisation's sustainable success.

The Innovative Communicator

An employee called Mike was, unbeknown to David, having financial problems. In fact all told, it was a difficult time for Mike who had been with the company for barely a year. He felt very fortunate to have his job and enjoyed it.

However like many people, with rising costs, a wife, a four-year-old son and another child on the way, money was tight and Mike was struggling to make ends meet. His financial woes came to a head when, with less than a month before the birth of his second child, it became clear that the family could not all share the one room they called home since moving back to Britain, having lived abroad for some years. They had found a small suitable flat to rent but soon discovered that they needed references and a £1400 deposit. Mike confided his situation to a work colleague who immediately mentioned that the company, under David's leadership, had set up a special benevolent fund under a charitable trust, which was there to deal with existing and past employees in the industry who had fallen on hard times. The friend advised and encouraged Mike to talk to his line manager. Mike did. Within a few days Mike's circumstances were assessed. He was given a reference for the estate agent and the £1400 needed to secure the flat which was to be his new home.

He felt strongly he wanted to show his gratitude to the man who had made this possible. As a result of the open-door policy David operated in the business, Mike genuinely felt he was able to make an appointment to meet the CEO. David is a CEO who connects personally with his people because he makes it his business to do so on a regular and consistent basis.

Mike went with his wife to meet David to thank him. He told me that in his private half-hour meeting with David, he was at one point overcome with emotion because without that £1400 he and his wife and children would have been homeless. David had been gracious and kind to them in that private meeting. He talked with them at length and with depth and meaning, Mike added.

Mike's manager went on to tell me that while Mike had always been hard working he had "completely upped his game" since becoming a beneficiary of the company's benevolent fund in his hour of need. The manager added that since the incident two years previously, Mike had *continued to be "a worker on steroids". His loyalty and dedication to the company was highly evident and the CEO had played a major part in that.*

In describing why they stayed with the company and enjoyed working there, the employees would consistently mention the CEO, David. They were fired up in a positive way by the way he treated them, by how they felt genuinely valued by him for their efforts on behalf of the business he leads, for his tough but fair ways, for his genuine generosity of spirit and for the way in which he actively engages with them through good, meaningful, effective communication. Significantly, they said they believe him when he speaks to them. They frequently said "he doesn't spin us a corporate line".

They all said what they valued most about him was his ability to communicate with them regardless of how busy he is.

Miranda and David work in completely different businesses which operate on completely different scales. Yet both have got things right and achieved sustainable success. Their achievements have been very largely down to clear, honest, meaningful communication which puts their employees and customers at the heart of their business.

> **What Miranda and David have in common is that they do not pay lip-service to the idea of good communication, they deliver it.**

What has been going wrong?

In the Introduction to this book I outlined what's going wrong in large businesses today, and why good people-communication is so important for lasting success. Here's a summary of these crucial main points:

- Globalisation means demand for lower costs and faster delivery.

- Globalisation means frenetic change is the norm.

- Frenetic change includes mergers, acquisitions, takeovers, downsizing and redundancies.

- Fast-track profit at all cost is endemic.

- Priority has moved from *people, process, technology* to *technology, process, people.* This often results in bad communication between people.

- Bad communication leaves employees and customers disgruntled, cynical, suspicious, misunderstood and distrustful.

- Unhappy employees impact negatively on production and profits.

- Bad communication is bad business.

The Edelman Survey

In January 2012, the world's largest independent Public Relations Agency, Edelman, produced its prestigious Edelman Trust Barometer Annual Global Study.

The survey revealed that "only 30% of UK respondents found CEO's to be believable spokespeople for their organisation."

"This plunge, 9% down from the previous survey, compares with a 25% rise in the credibility of 'people like yourself', taking this category up to 60%."

As Danny Rogers, Editor in Chief of the respected communications industry magazine *PR Week* put it "This is pretty incredible. The very people running the companies are not regarded as credible."

Edelman's twelfth annual survey showed that only 38% of people trusted business to do the right thing, while 72% believed companies should be involved in solving social and environmental problems. *Credit Source: Edelman 2012 Trust Barometer/PR Week*

There is clearly an apparent crisis of trust and confidence facing business leaders. The brutal fact is: trust in business remains "wrecked". Ed Williams, Chief Executive Officer of Edelman UK says "Trust in CEOs has slipped further with people trusting almost every other type of spokesperson higher than the boss. The CEO is now one of the most distrusted authority figures. The challenge for business is that to become more trusted – to move from simply protecting its "licence to operate to establishing a licence to lead – it needs to move beyond operational excellence to address society's priorities."

Ed Williams adds "One of the key findings in the survey was that large numbers of the public expect business to do much more than just make money and create jobs.

They expect business to improve the world it operates in for the better, act ethically, treat employees well and help local communities."

> *In the tough political and economic climate where chaos is rife, business leaders can no longer expect an automatic 'licence to lead', simply because of who they are.*

They have to work for it and earn it and are expected to do so by their people and the public. They will be judged by the substance of their actions and their meaningful communication of them.

What the UK public thinks

> Just **30%** of UK respondents found CEOs to be believable spokespeople for their organisation
>
> Just **18%** of those polled believed business placed customers ahead of profits
>
> Just **11%** said the Government communicated frequently and honestly
>
> While **68%** believed the UK was heading on the wrong track
>
> While **58%** of respondents trusted TV and radio news
>
> Credit source: Edelman Trust Barometer 2012

So what does it take to be that "believable spokesperson"? What does it take to bring in profits, and have happy staff and customers? What does it take to feel you are "on the right track"?

Enter the Innovative Communicator

This book is about being a communication leader of choice. You too can become an Innovative Communicator if you wish. If you choose to, it will transform your business.

Innovative – because they think outside the box as the norm, they do things differently, they are bold, and they are inspirational. They combine this with a deep grounding in common sense but are not afraid to push their own boundaries.

They are adept at building great relationships, collaboration and getting people involved and are not afraid or averse to looking for opportunities to bring a humanity into their dealings. They manage to get others excited about buying into positive new ideas and methods, and in doing so often transform the way people think. Their skills generate belief and enthusiasm about goals and the actions needed to achieve those goals. Practical action backs their vision. They are clear thinkers and strong decision makers.

Communicator – because through their style of language (both verbal and body language) which is honest, warm and approachable, they engage the receiver. They strongly believe in a people-centred strategy to deliver clear bold, effective communication with eyeball-to-eyeball contact between people as the cornerstone for communicating key messages and major news (sometimes grim news). This done with integrity, respect and heart is the corner-stone and success to their business. They inspire. They are role models.

Does this person actually exist? What my studies showed

In 2009, I put myself though rigorous professional training (one must do this regularly as a communication professional) and during the six-month course, I had to come up with a communication project to research and write.

January 2009 was just months after the global banking crises of November 2008, and out of the ashes of the debacle, I could see that the delivery of effective communication in business – now more important than ever – would need to be delivered differently. That difference needed to be specifically suited to a climate of on-going business chaos in order to successfully assist and deliver business success.

I came to realise that business as usual (BAU) will almost inevitably become "history". The context in which people-communication now operates is frenetic, fast, moving, changing and chaotic. Businesses need to come to terms with this fact quickly.

> *I was fascinated to explore what would make the difference in organisations in this new acerbic and difficult era. So, the project I came up with was: "How organisations re-invent themselves to become leaders of the new way".*

It was during my research for this work that I came across specific individuals who stood head-and-shoulders above their peers in making a difference through the power of their unique and offbeat communication skills within their organisation.

I noted the huge priority they placed on communication, innovating, introducing new ideas or refreshing and reinventing past ideas, using their intuition and re-adapting communication in their business appropriately to enable real achievement of goals. Above all, they didn't just talk about the importance they placed on communication and then pay lip service to it, thereby producing a chasm between rhetoric and actuality (the biggest problem for most organisations). Instead, these individuals believed the actions of effective communication every day, was the way forward. The results of their daily behaviour had dynamic results on their businesses.

I researched completely different but equally successful organisations in terms of how their collective workforce were genuinely made to feel Inclusive, and therefore in turn made a real contribution to business goals.

> *I noticed that the individuals who ignited this collective feeling of inclusiveness in the workforce through their communication skills, had a range of very similar characteristics and attributes.*

The Innovative Communicator

Henry's core values

One of the people I was privileged to interview was a global leader of a major organisation which, under his leadership spanning thirteen years, has become the epitome of how a large organisation should be run. We'll call him Henry.

During Henry's leadership the organisation has gone from local to national and then global success with a presence in over 200 countries. This organisation amongst other things is particularly successful at running courses at a time when many of its competitors have struggled to do the same.

As a global CEO, two things immediately struck me about Henry – his humility, (a genuine absence of inappropriate ego) and the top priority he places on putting people at the heart of the business combined with the role communication plays in making this happen. He is also keenly active in the development and delivery of the organisation's overall communication strategy.

As a man who views himself as under authority (to those he ultimately reports to) as well as in authority, Henry strongly believes that his role as a leader is to find the right people for his leadership team, build great relationships with them by communicating and connecting with them in a meaningful way (as we will see) and that this then enables them to be their best, to release their energy and talent to make the difference. They too become leaders and Henry, as an inspirational communicator, has been their role model.

Henry meets with his leadership team of fifteen people every week for three hours. Significantly, the first hour is always spent on one question: "How are you?". The first hour is dedicated to as he puts it "What's going on in their lives". The remaining two hours is then a forum to discuss issues, and for the team to express their strong opinions and diversity of views which is firmly encouraged. He believes people should say what they think so they can talk about it together (rather than people feeling unable to do so in a collective and bottling their true opinions). Henry says he is very reliant on his team and believes he is only as good as his team.

Meet the Innovative Communicator

Henry pointed out that the success of the organisation has evolved from a nurturing of the "tribe" and that he does everything possible to protect that genuine sense of community. To do this he points out that you have to constantly talk and 'have conversations' with your people. He does this with his team, their teams and front line staff as well as customers. He adds: "We take a holistic approach to the whole of life. The workplace is where people are most of the time, so it is about the mobilisation of everyone. You need effective strong communication between people to do this. That's why our community events, coffee sessions, getting together with food to interact, sharing ideas both formally and informally, getting to know each other better and continuously building our day to day relationships is so important."

As a business, he and his leadership team are looking for, and impart, three key values when recruiting staff. Capability, integrity, and the ability or willingness to learn to communicate in a way that is beneficial to the wider community. He believes the quality of content and its effective communication feeds understanding, so as a business they work very hard at this. This gives people an experience that is relevant and memorable for the right reasons.

They constantly talk to their customers refining their business to meet their customers' needs. They change the order and emphasis of their talks and courses as well as their marketing of them in direct response to feedback.

They know for instance that a telephone system which relies on voice activation as opposed to human beings would not be right for their own staff or customers, so they avoid it. Their phone system ensures that after the initial recorded voice message to direct your call to the appropriate area, a human being from the right area receives your call immediately to speak to. People appreciate this, it matters to Henry that they do and it's important and productive for the business, because they know from their research that they retain customers in this way.

The business also has a lay group of staff and customers who give feedback and help run the business on the front line, so if Henry misses something or something isn't right, his leadership team who have their ears to the ground will pick it up on his behalf.

The Innovative Communicator

To reach a wider audience Henry has done so by writing several best-selling books which have sold millions of copies world wide. He is a highly sought-after international speaker. His ethos is that it is important for his organisation to play its part in the transformation of society. This ethos drives their success.

Henry is a role-model of a leader with excellent communication skills and these skills are strongly promoted in the work culture. He has an effective way of getting ideas across, simplifies things (avoids jargon) and uses metaphors. He has strong interpersonal skills, is articulate and eloquent. His body language, of which communication plays a significant part, is one of authentic strength, charismatic leadership, poise, calm, thoughtfulness, inclusivity and belief in purpose.

Key qualities of the Innovative Communicator – summary

The table below is a summary of the qualities I observed in the highly successful individuals that I was privileged to meet and know. Their qualities inspired me to develop the concept of the Innovative Communicator.

Throughout the book we will see a wider range of qualities, which will be summarised at the end of each chapter.

An Innovative communicator:

Has the ability to re-invent and innovate in a constantly changing environment in a way that is good for business

Is bold – does things differently while staying grounded in common sense

Is good at building relationships; engenders loyalty

Is good at getting people involved, collaborative

Generates enthusiasm in others to new ideas or doing things differently

Is practical – action backs vision and ideas

Creates, spots, seizes and acts on opportunities

Is a strong thinker, clear decision maker

Is passionate about face-to-face communication being a cornerstone vehicle in strategy wherever possible

Has the ability to think strategically and plan tactically and operationally with people at the heart and focus

Pushes own boundaries. Will try something new, will take a deep breath and action!

> Is curious, caring, a listener, intuitive, focussed and courageous
>
> Will do what is right, will persevere
>
> Is engaging. Able to persuade, influence and secure the commitment of others particularly in difficult circumstances
>
> Is committed, resourceful, operates well under pressure
>
> Is a motivated self-starter, who also works well as part of a team
>
> Is a big fan of clarity. Quick to assimilate complex information, make sense of it and make it accessible and simple for others to understand
>
> Believes the cup is always half full rather than half empty. Looks on the bright side of life. Enthusiasm, smiles and generosity of spirit
>
> Has the personality mix of a good project manager with discipline and structure combined with flexibility, spontaneity and get up and go!

Questions to think about

- Have you ever experienced the qualities of the Innovative Communicator in anyone in your life? It could have been an employer, a teacher at school, or someone you looked up to.

- Do you recognise any of the Innovative Communicator qualities above in yourself?

- In your business, no matter what it is, do you feel you have a vision for how you could be making a difference?

- Do you believe that what you do is part of something bigger, and has a wider benefit?

- Do you "really love" what you do?

- Are you comfortable with taking a calculated risk to try something different?

- Do you place value on communicating with integrity and honesty?

- Do you place a priority on motivating and appreciating your staff or team members?

- Have you created ways to encourage and inspire your staff or team members?

- Do you show (rather than just tell) your staff or team members that they are your most valuable resource?

- Can you imagine the added value to your business if both you and your staff or team members could discover, identify and fully use your best communication skills?

Exercise

If you do one thing today, think back to people who have influenced you positively as role models – whether it was teachers, employers, colleagues, friends or family – and make a mental note of what communication qualities those people had and the effect they had.

2

Build deep relationships

> *"The bedrock of a great business is based on human capital and that capital is built on human relationships."*
> **Miti Ampoma**

Martha's two banks

Martha has two banks, both are well-known large organisations. One is for her personal banking, while the other is for her business banking. She has a telephone banking service with both banks and that sadly is where the similarity ends. She describes her relationship with the two banks as "chalk and cheese". She has a strong relationship with one bank with a huge sense of loyalty towards them. "As long as they are this good, I'll never leave them," she says. She adds "I've been with them for almost fifteen years and I often think, if only they had a business banking service, I'd leave my business bank like a shot!"

Of her business bank resentment and resigned weariness instantly descends in her voice "I dread speaking to them. I have to psyche myself up, it's such a dreadful experience. It takes forever to get through, they never return calls if they say they will and you just sense it's utter chaos all the time. The left never seems to know what the right is doing. The problem is I feel they don't care about me and I'm just another statistic. There's no point leaving them for another one, because I've spoken with my friends who are spread amongst the others. There's not much choice and all our experiences are the same. No point jumping from the frying pan into the fire."

Build deep relationships

So what is it that makes Martha have two such starkly contrasting experiences with two organisations in the same industry? Martha was straight out with the answer "It's the way they communicate with me, or not, in the case of my business bank. It's the way they make me feel. I come off the phone exhausted and dissatisfied more often than not and you know there's no point filling in their endless customer satisfaction surveys because they don't take any notice. If they did they wouldn't have the same dreadful service year after year. I feel trapped because I need a business bank and that's why I'm with them, not because I want to be."

This is a typical conversation that Martha has with her business bank as she starts the process to speak to a human being (her "Relationship Manager" and the only service that can help):

The phone rings at least ten times, sometimes more before the bank's voice activator (BVA) responds:

BVA: Welcome to the Bank of Dread, please say or key in your account number now.
M: punch, punch, punch, punch, punch, punch . . .
BVA: And your six digit sort code.
M: punch, punch, punch, punch, punch, punch . . .
BVA: Please say or key in your date of birth using a six digit format.
M: punch, punch, punch, punch, punch, punch . . .
BVA: You'll now be asked to speak two of the characters from your password, for example A for Alpha or B for Brava. Please say the first character of your password now.
M: M.
BVA: Is that M?
M: Yes.
BVA: And the sixth character.
M: Q.
BVA: Is that Q?
M: Yes.
BVA: Thanks, answering "Yes" or "No", do you want to hear your balance?
M: No.
BVA: OK. You can now say recent transactions or press one, transfers and payments two, use a different account three, or another service four.

The Innovative Communicator

M: Another service.
BVA: Thanks. Please say direct debits or press one, standing orders two, balance three, change security number four, or advisor five.
M: Advisor.
BVA: Please hold for an advisor.

A voice recording: Please be aware that your call may be recorded for training purposes. You will now be connected to the next available advisor.

"The above process takes anything up to five minutes, sometimes more, depending on how long the phone has rung unanswered. Having got through the voice activation process, you may have to wait another five minutes or much longer, as is often the case, for an advisor to come on. They then have to take you through another security process, before wanting to know your tale, which they are not empowered to help you with, before eventually putting you on hold to go and find a Relationship Manager (because you never get the same person) and this may take another five minutes. Before I actually get the service I need, I can have been on that phone for up to half an hour, sometimes more, just trying to get through. I feel tired just thinking about it. The communication is so frustrating," says Martha.

In contrast, here is Martha's experience of her personal telephone banking. She immediately perks up and smiles. "I love them," she says. "They are so personable and approachable. It's not that things haven't gone wrong in the past. When they have, they treat me fairly and put things right immediately if it's been their fault. They are fantastic.

I simply ring the telephone number and within five rings a lovely warm human voice will say":

Voice: Good afternoon Ms Smith. This is Beth from the Happy Bank, may I take your surname and postcode please?
M: Smith, SW1 457.
Beth: And your date of birth?
M: 5th September 1958.
Beth: Can I take the first digit of your password?
M: W.
Beth: And the last digit

M: Q.
Beth: And finally your place of birth.
M: Italy.
Beth: *[In a genuine warm friendly caring tone]* And how may I help you today Ms Smith?

"It's such a relief and a great contrast. They sort out what I need, we finish with a short, cheery chat about whatever is going on, and I'm left with a great feeling that I matter to the people who have my money. Why can't my other bank do this?" says Martha perplexed

Martha's experience is familiar to all of us. I challenge you to show me someone who has not, in recent years, felt like shouting into their phone "I just want to speak to a person!".

In the words of Swami BV Narayana who compiled the book *Kitchen of Love,* "Technology can be great. It makes for a more efficient life. However as our world becomes more technology-driven, we also crave authentic experiences. If technology supports our relationships, then all is well. If it gets in the way, then our lives can be poorer".

As human beings we are made for relationships. It is a fundamental human need to communicate via language and speech, an authentic experience many people crave in a business world of increasingly soulless voice-activated speech, pin numbers and passwords.

Our need for human relationships and human communication is why we have friends, families, loved ones and other relationships of choice. It is our interdependency and true connections with other human beings that makes us feel valued and helps us flourish. This is equally true of the relationships and bonds we form and develop and are recipients of in the workplace. The power of these relationships is precious and priceless.

> ***Building deep relationships, nurturing them, guarding them closely and watching over them all the time, every time, lies at the root and centre of outstanding people-communication programmes. This is what really makes a difference to the bottom line of performance in business.***

What do we mean by a deep relationship in business?

- Where each person feels known
- Where each person feels valued
- Where each person feels they are trusted
- Where each person feels they can trust
- Where each person feels they are supported
- Where each person feels a participant and involved in the decision-making process
- Where each person feels their ideas and contributions count
- Where each person 'buys' into the organisational philosophy voluntarily
- Where moral is high

Put simply, deep relationships that work are the key to success. They put *people* at the centre rather than systems or technology. Without valued and motivated people, an organisation – no matter how great its methodologies, processes and variety of communication channels – is likely to go nowhere fast. This may or may not seem obvious. The fact is most organisations don't build deep relationships, and if they do, they do it badly.

The benefits

Once we have established deep relationships where there is trust and respect, it means that:

- People are able to have honest conversations in the right place at the right time.
- People and issues are not ignored or swept under the carpet. Important views that need to be aired and discussions that need to be had, happen in a safe and supportive environment.

Build deep relationships

- People are *happy* to have difficult conversations – a key ingredient for success. Sparks may fly, disagreements may ensue, but the outcome is worth it for the greater good.

  The depth of the relationship that allows the successful outcome can withstand the difficult conversation or awkward situation.

- A deep relationship will grow further and richer during or after a difficult conversation and most certainly after a positive outcome for the greater good, as a result of the difficult conversation. This is the measure and sign of a mature, healthy relationship with depth.

- Each individual relationship nurtured, developed and continued will build collective confidence, team spirit and the feeling for the majority that 'we are all in it together'. This momentum builds and becomes self-perpetuating.

- Everyone then wants to be involved in being part of the solution.

- This in turn creates ambassadors for the business and once that happens it's hello world, we *are* the business!

How the Innovative Communicator builds deep relationships

- ***An Innovative Communicator makes the time and effort to find out who their people are***

  It may sound obvious, but sadly many senior executives and managers in big business are so removed from their people, they have little or no idea of who they are as human beings. In an environment of change and perhaps chaos, the Innovative Communicator will seek to know the truth, people's views and perspectives especially on what their change journey actually means for them.

  As an Innovative Communicator, you can get to know information such as:

  - What someone did before they joined the organisation

- What makes them tick as a person

- What they are passionate about in life

- What they are less keen on

I remember once going to talk to a man in the mailroom of a large organisation I was working at. The mailroom and its staff, which he led, were impacted by major changes. I contacted him and arranged to meet him. My main reason for the meeting was simply to meet him, allow us to put a face to each other, and listen and talk.

In an hour of chatting and listening, it transpired that this man came from a military background, which couldn't have been further from the world of mailroom employees he led in the organisation we both found ourselves in.

I knew that one of the very senior management also came from a similar military background. I mentioned this to both men and their subsequent relationship, cemented by their mutual background and history in the army, meant that a great deal of progress was made on business plans for the mailroom employees which included some tough decisions.

> **Their similar background, which they were unaware of before I found out and mentioned it to them, was instrumental in their working relationship, which was in turn instrumental in the successful outcome for the business.**

That initial hour of chatting was worth its weight in gold.

- **Innovative Communicators develop unique bonds with individuals**

  You'll be amazed at what you have in common with another person and what they are passionate about in life, if you take the time to listen to them and pick up on what is really going on in their world. Whatever they are passionate or feel strongly about is a key plank and starting point in building an effective working relationship between you and them.

As well as finding out about their background, you need to be listening for things like:

- What you have in common with the other person, what you both agree on and what brings you together.

- What you respect and admire about each other.

- What you both feel brings a special and unique quality to the relationship.

Everyone understands the need for this commonality, for the good and progress of working through the inevitably tough work challenges you are jointly embarking on together.

I remember a particularly challenging change and transformation programme, working closely as the communication head with project managers on geographically spread sites across the country. On our two toughest sites, I had excellent relationships with both project managers, so that we mutually went the extra mile for each other to ensure the outcome was brilliant for the business.

The quality of my relationships was not down to luck. In nurturing and building those two relationships with two entirely different personalities, I discovered that one project manager was a very talented award-winning photographer in his spare time, whilst the other project manager was a successful kinesiology practitioner in her spare time. In my spare time, I have a love of the arts and photography and ended up visiting this project managers exhibitions which meant we became friends, and as I am also an experienced clinical massage therapist in my spare time, the other project manager and I became equally good friends as we shared a love for complementary medicine.

These deep relationships meant we would go the extra mile for each other, we were able to do a superlative job for the client and organization in a particularly tough climate, overcoming many challenges.

- ***Innovative Communicators really listen to what is under the surface***

Having built rapport, discovered what you have in common with another person and made an initial bond, every individual wants to feel heard and respected. This is achieved through listening. Listening to another person enables them to fully express their thoughts, hopes and fears. It also shows them that you have heard their cry, if they have one. It is vital to listen well. You need to be listening for:

- What motivates them about the job they do and what doesn't.

- What worries them about the changes.

- What their underlying niggles are, things that aren't priority worries, but nag them nevertheless.

- What they would like to see happen for the good of everyone and the business.

I remember working on a challenging programme where job-role changes and impending redundancies business-wide had been announced. The employees on the programme felt lucky to have secured jobs on the particular programme we were on, as they watched their colleagues face an uncertain future.

As the months went by I noticed one employee whom I had built a strong relationship with, didn't seem quite herself. When I initially asked her if she was alright, she'd respond that she was fine. As my relationship with her deepened, we had a café lunch at which I mentioned that I was worried about her, as I sensed all was not well. I told her I was happy to listen if she needed to talk. A few days later she came to me. She had had major back problems the year before which she had kept quiet about and overcome. However it meant that constant pressure on her back was an issue. Her newly secured role in the business required her to constantly travel and help move furniture around. She was terrified of aggravating her back and her health but equally terrified of losing her job if she said anything, due to the business climate of fear and insecurity. She didn't want to talk to her manager, who was likely to lose his job too and she didn't want to talk to the HR helpline available because she had "no relationship with HR or the stranger at the end of the phone". However her predicament was really affecting her.

I sought and got her permission to sensitively discuss her situation with her manager as I knew he really cared about his team despite his own uncertain future. I did so. As she was very good at her job, the manager, and the business, didn't want to lose her. The result was that she was moved to a role which involved a lot less travel and no moving of furniture. It was a win-win for everyone in the business.

- **Innovative Communicators intuitively spot opportunities, times and places, to begin to build relationships**

The office desk and meeting rooms are NOT the territory. They are not the only place or necessarily the best place to build deep relationships. The Innovative Communicator understands this.

The best places in the office building include the canteen (for those businesses that still have them) or office cafés, coffee time, lunchtime get-togethers, the after work evening drink, organised or impromptu social gatherings.

- The first time could simply be a friendly smile as you pass in the corridor, waiting for the lift or meeting by chance in the loo!

- The next time might be the smile and stop for a quick chat.

- A third encounter might be a smile, a stop for a chat and the spontaneous committed agreement to pop some time in the diary to spend some quality time over a topic of mutual interest.

I can speak for women here when I say, milestone moments in relationships are carved over slapping on some lippy and adjusting make-up in the ladies loos. Long live these opportunities.

I remember a programme where a recently joined project manager I needed to work with was struggling to keep me in the loop on communication issues – a tad vital, given I was leading the communication programme. As the weeks rolled on, I could feel my irritation rising as gentle reminders went unheeded. It got to the point where I knew my next step would make or break our relationship and therefore in some part at least, the future success of the programme. I needed to take action and find the common denominator between us.

A few days later I was working late in the office when I noticed the project manager was too. I went and said hello, chatted for a while and spontaneously asked her if she had eaten and if not did she fancy a drink and a bite to eat. She enthusiastically jumped at the offer.

> **A social one-to-one evening over olives, bread and wine transformed our working relationship in one stroke. We had a great evening, found we had loads in common, shared a colossal sense of humour and laughed a lot.**

From that next day, we had an unspoken bond and physiology of warmth, laughter and mutual respect. We went on to work very well and closely together and delivered a project for the client to be proud of.

The bottom line is collectively, these opportunities used well, will form friendships and mutual respect which influence and make a difference to business goals and outcomes, because it is the way in which people deliver those goals and outcomes that matters and makes a difference in your business. That difference is rooted in deep relationships between work colleagues.

- **Innovative Communicators allow time for the relationship to develop**

Building a deep relationship can't be done overnight. Timing is everything as you are developing trust and warmth. Take each step at a time. Create building blocks. There is a structure and a protocol involved.

- When you start, a smile and a short conversation will do. Don't be a gushing evangelist on day one!

Build deep relationships

- Pick up the phone to make the next relevant appointment where you can, rather than send an email. When you speak on the phone, you can then agree to send a calendar invite.

- The conversation you've already had will have added another layer of appropriate familiarity – and it matters. If you are on one of those many dial-in calls week in and week out, where there are particular individuals you would benefit from getting to know better, make it a point to develop those relationships beyond the weekly (or otherwise) dial-in calls.

- Make a list of five to eight key people you need to get to know better each week and make a commitment to call them on the phone, have a conversation and pop a date in the diary to meet to discuss the work at hand face-to-face. If they are at another site or area, find out when they are coming to your neck of the woods and vice versa and book a time for then, so you are keeping within business budgets.

- Make yourself accountable to follow through this task. By doing this, you will find within a short space of time that the quality of your relationships and the results they generate in the business turns heads in your workforce for the right reasons.

- Be consistent in your efforts and keep going. This work is not a one effort wonder.

I once worked in a business where the reputation of someone preceded them, unfortunately for all the wrong reasons. When I joined the team I was warned that the person was very difficult to get on with. She was viewed as scary, distant and unhelpful. For right or wrong this perception was a strong one amongst key members of the team I was working with.

The issue, as I saw it, was that it would be good for our team to have her on side if we possibly could, given the role she had in the business. As I was new to the team, I promptly made a half hour face-to-face appointment to visit her myself. Within ten minutes we had found common ground on hobbies and interests. I listened a lot to what she felt passionate about, which clearly invigorated her.

Once I sensed we had reached a good place rapport-wise, I turned the conversation to our work, asking her to share her views on the status quo. I then shared my potential plans for the programme, and made it clear that her views would be most appreciated as we worked on rolling them out.

Far from being the scary, distant character that had been portrayed, she was wholly engaged adding that she'd be pleased to help and contribute wherever she could. Over the next three months, I paced and built our relationship step-by-step, in a consistent way, forwarding on ideas and plans and including her in appropriate invitations. If I felt I hadn't heard from her for a few weeks, I'd send a quick email simply asking how she and her team were. I'd always get a response.

Gradually she began reciprocating, contacting me and suggesting ways in which her team could collaborate with mine on an on-going basis. We then agreed to have diarised structured weekly catch-up meetings for our team members and a one-to-one equivalent for the two of us. These took place without fail. The key sceptics in my team thawed, especially when they worked with her team members whom they got on with really well.

After about six weeks the two of us did a "cheap and cheerful" lunch which was a hybrid of a working one and catching up on the latest news of our respective mutual hobbies and interests. Within three months, she was totally on side and our joints efforts on behalf of the business were the better for our harmonious and effective working relationship.

A happy postscript: *A couple of years after I had finished working at this business, the person mentioned contacted me to let me know that they had decided to emigrate to Australia. We have kept in touch since and whenever I visit Australia, where I have many friends, she has invited me to visit her, as a friend, in her very different lifestyle there.*

Build deep relationships

- ***Innovative Communicators operate with Diplomacy, Discretion, Trust and Integrity (DDTI)***

    As an Innovative Communicator you will inevitably "know" all kinds of confidential information and need to uphold an unrivalled reputation for diplomacy, discretion, trust and integrity.

    Programme team members, as well as the impacted parties you have built strong relationships with, will confide in you about all sorts of things from corridor conversations, gossip, rumours circulating the grape vine, to indiscretions, and politically-charged clangers which are best left alone. People know that what they wish to stay private will remain private when they confide in you. This includes having a moan and letting off steam about other colleagues and they do this confident in the knowledge that it won't go any further. But above all you will be given key essential golden nuggets of business information (you will often be the first to receive 'breaking news hot off the press') that, used wisely, creates vital, often extraordinary, shifts for the business and helps it achieve its transformational goals.

    - Whatever you are told as a confidante, you must keep as a confidante.

    - You should listen while staying as neutral and objective as possible.

    - You need to absorb the information and empathise where appropriate.

    - You should not speak ill or agree with any ill-speaking of others.

    - You do not repeat gossip or pass on or spread unsolicited information.

    - You use the golden nuggets of breaking news you receive diplomatically and wisely, to create organisational shifts for the greater good.

> **By practicing DDTI, an Innovative Communicator becomes known as 'the rock', someone that everyone can trust and talk to honestly and uninhibited, because they can be themselves.**

DDTI enables the Innovative Communicator to build deep relationships with people in order to get to the truth of the business. Once you have discovered the truth of the business (and this is not the corporate vision statement!) you can create and build an effective, tailor-made, people-to-people, communication programme that will resonate with impacted parties and help transform your business.

I worked in a business where in the last six months before they were due to leave as a result of downsizing, staff were recognised and praised by the managers of the business for their 100% unwavering commitment and professionalism till their last day. However in writing them a 'goodbye and thank you letter' and in nominating a manager to come personally on the last day to say farewell, management had agreed these duties should be carried out by a manager who was unanimously disliked, had rarely been around during these employees challenging change journey and whom many felt had "stirred up trouble and added fuel to fire" on frequent occasions when there was no need. In short they strongly felt he had not been there for them and didn't care.

I knew all this, because I had attended a formally structured, small but significant meeting about the lessons that could be learnt from how the change and transformation journey to the eventual loss of their jobs had been handled, in the eighteen months since they were told of their impending job losses and worked their notice. Those giving the lessons were a cross-section of the impacted people leaving the business including managers and team leaders. The strength of feeling about the inadequacy of the particular manager in question was left in no doubt. They made it clear they wanted nothing to do with him. So when their goodbye letter was being prepared with the individual's name on it, with a view that he would be the manager to wave them goodbye in person on their final day (some of them had over twenty years of company service) I knew it would be received very badly, indeed on a near mutiny scale. This kind of situation is not only grim for the exiting staff, but equally grim with the likelihood of a serious adverse effect on remaining staff and therefore the business itself.

Armed with this sensitive information I aimed to diffuse a potentially damaging scene on the final day of exit, by planning quickly to prevent it happening. I contacted the said manager's regional manager whom the staff did like. They had spoken warmly of her hard work and visible efforts on their behalf during the lessons learnt session. I diplomatically explained the situation to her and she agreed that it was best that the 'goodbye and thank you' letter was signed by her and that she attend in person to say goodbye. I left it with her. I kept the unhappy information to myself with the exception of the person I reported to. On the final day of the staff exit, a letter from the regional manager was well received and her presence in person was appreciated. All was well with staff who were leaving and with their colleagues who were staying.

- **The Innovative Communicator communicates "authentically"**

  What we mean by being "authentic":

  - There is a genuine and undisputed trustworthiness of character and behavior in a person that greatly appeals to others.

  - You feel that person wants to do the very best they can for you, with no hidden agendas.

  - They are transparent, open and honest in their dealings and interaction with others.

  - They pass the litmus test of "would I trust this person to pilot my plane" with flying colours because you believe they will be with you through thick and thin.

  - You believe they would go the extra mile to deliver for you because of who they are.

  - Authenticity in a human being is a powerful attraction to others and a great quality to have in abundance in a business.

- ***An Innovative Communicator feels the changes that are required for others***

  According to scientist, author and speaker Dr David Hamilton PhD "Empathy has been defined in the scientific journals as 'I feel with you.'" He says "With empathy, we share another's pain and we are very aware of the effect of our actions on them." As an Innovative Communicator, you will proactively build deep, effective, strong, working relationships with all impacted parties. To do this successfully you need to make it your business to understand and feel the changes that are required for others. This cannot be an academic exercise. And yes, "all impacted people" can be a lot of people, but that's what you need to do. It is time consuming, hard work and worth it.

  You should get to know your team leaders, in particular of your front-line staff. Through them, you will gain legitimate access to front-line teams. The relationships you build here are equally as important as the relationships you build with your executive and management colleagues.

  Remember real success comes from being a personal exemplar of the expertise you profess. It is not enough to preach it and strategise.

  > ***People need to see the authenticity of your behaviour, they need to see that you feel and understand the impact of the changes they are going through and are with them, offering and giving them active tangible support all the way.***

  I worked with a company who were undergoing major transformation of both their systems and their people at some considerable pace. Changes were happening particularly fast in two separate geographical locations where the plan was to close one office and relocate its people to the other. Both offices were named after their geographical areas, so let's just say one was called for example, the Solihull office while the other was called the Camberley office.

Build deep relationships

As the weeks went by, the Solihull office that was being closed down started to be suddenly called by a strange unfamiliar name. Managers had stopped calling it by its normal name of the Solihull office, and instead had combined the first few letters in that office name with the first few letters of the Camberley office that people were to move to in due course. Out of the blue, the Solihull office began to be called Solcam! The office staff in Solihull, including their local managers, made it very clear they immensely disliked this sudden peculiar amalgam and emergence of their unofficial new name. Yet no one took notice.

As the weeks went by, the new name spread and grew in use in proportion to the increasing resentment of the office staff. They responded by becoming visibly less engaging and co-operative about the practical changes that were required of them. Relationships with programme managers who had introduced Solcam grew increasingly tetchy. I placed the issue as a communication item agenda for discussion at the main programme team meeting, where I made an impassioned plea and case for restoring the original Solihull name the office was given, and losing the unofficial name amalgam as quickly as possible, in the interest of restoring and maintaining much needed goodwill. Goodwill was essential, given the huge changes that needed to be delivered with the help of affected staff. Mercifully, my plea was heeded. Solcam was dropped and the Solihull name and goodwill were restored.

An Innovative Communicator is not viewed as one of the many *leaders* of the business paying lip service to "improving communication with their people". They are different because they add real value and something extra by understanding people at a deeper level, connecting people with each other, saying what they mean and meaning what they say, and above all delivering powerful *enabling* communication which drives change whilst bringing people together to deliver the change for the greater good of the organisation.

> **Put simply, the impacted people an Innovative Communicator builds deep relationships with, believe in the Innovative Communicator.**

Creating and holding on to strong deep relationships with individuals across a business (especially a large one) is hard work. However, it is these critical relationships that see people getting to know each other as human beings as opposed to just people working at a desk day in and day out. This difference matters. Knowing each other, understanding a variety of views, embracing what is shared in common and respecting and giving space to differences, helps build great teams.

Great teams in turn go on to produce great ambassadors. In great ambassadors, you have a great business.

- **The Innovative Communicator knows how to handle the "organisational blocker"**

No organisation escapes the blocker. The person who appears to find something negative in every business goal or objective, moans endlessly about most things and stirs up trouble. In fact, the blocker can have genuine fears and concerns that may not be being heard. The blocker can be situated in the most critical positions. Blockers need to be listened to and it is crucial that you build a relationship with them.

- Do a little research among colleagues to find out what the blocker's interests and positive attributes are to help you begin to build a good relationship.

- Create and find opportunities to interact, however briefly – a smile and a "How are you?" as you pass in the corridor, a brief chat at a chance meeting.

- When you need to get in touch, do so by ringing and speaking to them, rather than emailing. Start the conversation after the initial pleasantries, with a fact found e.g. "I gather congratulations are in order with your winning first prize at the local marrow growing competition" or "Congratulations on your new-born daughter, what's her name?". Hear them beam with pride in response.

- Ask them to spare you ten to fifteen minutes of their time. Visit in person to talk.

- Do listen to their moans and gripes. View them as helpful insights into the problems and issues facing the business.

- Ask them insightful questions in response to their descriptions of what they see as problems. They love talking about themselves! It'll be great for rapport building.

- Once rapport is established gently influence an alternative perspective to the issues raised, connect and introduce them to others who might help resolve the problems and create solutions.

- Keep smiling and keep your sense of humour. It is simple, powerful, within your control and makes a big difference.

The difference deep relationships make

Picture this: a major blue chip British company with its business goal of completely transforming its IT function from being separate divisions into a centralised group shared-services model. The result was disruption and redundancies.

The company had tried to communicate their new business model to impacted parties using its IT senior management and its in-house team. It failed miserably. Evidence of failure was in the high attrition rate. Some of the best employees the business couldn't afford to, and didn't want to lose, were leaving at an alarming rate to competitors. The rumour mill was in overdrive, with plummeting moral resulting from employees feeling they were being kept in the dark about the substance and details behind the announced Shared Services.

When I joined to help as a communication specialist, I immediately discovered that the majority of impacted parties, including the majority of the workforce, had no idea of the organisation's plans for them. What had been communicated and what they had been told had been spun in corporate waffle and project speak as to make it unintelligible. Impacted colleagues were disaffected, cynical and suspicious. As far as they were concerned they were being told to be part of something they neither knew about nor understood. It was pretty shambolic and the task to "turn this juggernaut" around was a huge one.

The first deep relationship I built was with the man I worked for. I took the job on because I liked him on instinct. He was calm, tough but fair and realised that his organisation's in-house team were neither cutting the mustard or offering him the support he needed. He also recognised that an effective communication plan was vital, if he was to stop impacted colleagues haemorrhaging in disaffection any further. Within ten days I had located and talked face-to-face to key people, got them on side, got their support to talk to other members of their teams, got the real picture and reported back the truth of the problems. This gave me brownie points because these key people were feeding back to my new boss about how helpful I was. This in turn gave him some crucial quick wins. Building on this, I immediately put forward the idea of a regular news-letter and the planning of a roadshow.

The man who hired me did so on the brief of "Do what you need to do. I will back you all the way." And with that I set sail there and then, so to speak. So what did I do?

My first port of call was to the Head of Communication of the in-house team. As far as I was concerned, my job included getting to know them, getting them on side and persuading them that I was keen to work collaboratively. It was successful, and here is what we did.

Taking care not to tread on any toes

I suggested to my boss that I thought a monthly newsletter updating the entire group function was needed starting the month I joined; he was both ecstatic at the suggestion which he wholly agreed with, but utterly despondent that it would ever happen. The in-house team had never suggested it. But when he put my idea to them, despite them having twenty-five members in their team, they said they "didn't have the capacity to do it".

When I told him I could do it single-handed, he was incredulous and I am not entirely sure he believed me. When I wrote the first introductory bumper edition in ten days, having interviewed a variety of key players *across the business on all levels and got it ready in a template, he was speechless. All I needed now was to get the sign-off from the in-house Head of Communication. I wasn't obliged to do so at this stage because it had been signed off with the go ahead from executives who were delighted, but realising it was wise not to tread on any toes, I was very keen to keep the Head of Communication on side. I had designed the template and built in the company colours and logo. When the head saw it, she asked that the template be adjusted to accurately reflect the company's stricter guidelines in terms of design and company colours. Once I did this she was delighted, felt she had contributed and from then on, we became working friends. I kept her in the loop and we worked extremely well together. I am thankful that I am aware of how easy it is to tread on people's toes by not respecting them and their responsibilities. The newsletter was on a roll and a huge success.*

Uniting the teams – getting everyone on side

My next job was how to connect all impacted parties, spread across the country from Brighton to Edinburgh and for them to get the "we are all in this together" feeling in the muscle. A herculean task, I might add, in the circumstances I inherited.

For the first six weeks I spoke with, and where possible visited, all key managers and team leaders of impacted geographical sites, so I could understand and feel the level of challenge and change for myself, as well as build deep personal relationships. I got to know them, they got to know me, and we put faces to each other's names while spending time discussing our shared views and values. My travelling round the country was done in the name of building deep relationships and strong bonds.

I then suggested to my boss that key members of our programme team should go on a roadshow, where we would go to the people on their home turf and explain what the business was trying to do. What we also needed to do, I suggested, was to get senior executive members (EXCO) and senior management on board this roadshow to demonstrate their commitment to the programme.

To date, the feedback I had received overwhelmingly from impacted parties, particularly front line staff, whose work made a difference to the business, was that their senior executives and management were conspicuous by their absence. Not only did I think they should be visible on my proposed roadshow, I believed they should be visibly accountable by doing questions and answer sessions. Like so many corporate organisations, this one was no exception in telling their staff time and time again that as their senior management, they were committed to seeing them and treating them fairly, that they were all in it together, only for their behaviour to demonstrate the exact opposite.

The silver tongue of persuasion

As a communication professional, getting eight members of a corporations executive committee and a further eight senior executives to commit to the day and cause, within a four week period just before Christmas, is an outright challenge. It is one thing to think it, articulate it and want it to happen and quite another to achieve it. Within hours, I was on the phone building deep and charming relationships with executives' PAs to book me time in their boss's diaries. My immediate goal with the PAs was to pitch my requirements and promote the compelling "why I'd be indebted for an appointment in their busy diary" in under a minute in each case . . . and get the desired result. I got an appointment in all sixteen executive diaries within days.

Here is a typical phone conversation (I've changed the names of people and departments as you can imagine):

PA (Jill): Hello, Bob Sykes' office. Jill speaking. How may I help you?

Miti: [*Warm tone of voice*] Hello Jill, I do hope you can. My name is Miti and I work in Group IT.
[*If at this point I already know them, I'll just say "It's Miti and start the conversation with a mutual titbit of interest such as "Hi Jill it's, Miti, how are you? How was the charity bowling evening last week?"*]

Miti: I'm keeping everything crossed that you might be able to help me. I need a minor miracle at this point!

Jill: I'll try.

Build deep relationships

Miti: Well, I work for Alan Smith the Director. As you know the problem facing the business is the level of uncertainty and widespread unhappiness amongst staff since the announcement of the new Shared Services model. Lots of people are leaving and the management is concerned and wants to make communication a priority to help sort out the difficulties. Given the tight time-table, with just four weeks to go before Christmas, we need to plan the solutions before Christmas, so we can hit the ground running with them, as soon as we come back in the New Year. Frankly Jill, we need to achieve the challenging feat of getting the majority of staff, especially Business Analysts and Project Managers back on side. It means planning a sparkling communication programme that'll achieve this as soon as possible. To do this, the management team have agreed that a main solution is to go on a roadshow first thing in the new year. This will give them the opportunity to talk directly to people face-to-face on their work turf, build relationships, understand their difficulties and pain points, directly address their concerns and issues and provide appropriate solutions in an interactive environment. They want to add real substance to the roadshow solution with a series of films for it and of course the timeline for this is very tight! In a nutshell Jill, we need to film and produce three stylish DVDs featuring eight directors and eight senior managers talking for three to four minutes each, to show at all the sites across the country. The executives want the DVDs to form a central piece of the roadshow. They'd very much like Bob to feature in the DVD in his role as Director of Technical Delivery in terms of his key messages to people and what his division is aiming to achieve for the business.

Jill: Yes . . . mmm . . . yes . . . I see.

Miti: It's Christmas in four weeks' time . . . Yikes . . . you can see where I'm going with this!

Jill: *[Laughs]*

Miti: *[Tone of voice remains warm and empathetic]*
I'm organizing the filming schedule now for 8th of January.

	Mark, Henry, Sue and Mary's PA's have created miracles and they are scheduled in the diary for the day's filming. I was wondering whether there was a smidgen of hope that you might be able to find time in Bob's hectic schedule for him to be filmed on the same day.
Jill:	Hmm . . . ummm . . . How much time do you need?
Miti:	Approximately half an hour. Filming is in room 2A on the ground floor in this building, but if it helps we can come to Bob's office and do it.
Jill:	Umm, well, that would make life easier. He's booked solid all day, it'll be hard to fit that in . . . when would you want him?
Miti:	Late morning would be ideal, Jill, or about 4.30?
Jill:	Umm, let me see. I would have to move his 12.00 appointment which is less critical . . . . can't move that . . . he's got to be at this one . . . what about say 11.30 in the morning or 4.00 in the afternoon. I'll get him to come to you.
Miti:	Oh Jill you are a darling. I'll grab 11.30 in the morning with both hands. I'm hugging you over the phone now. Thank you so much.
Jill:	*[Laughs more]* No problem Miti. Glad I could help.
Miti:	I'll send you the filming schedule and some briefing notes. Can I just check your email address?
Jill:	Of course. *[She gives it]*
Miti:	Thanks again Jill. Really appreciate it. Email to follow right away.
Jill:	Look forward to it.
Miti:	Thanks. Take care.
Jill:	You too.

I found the combination of a friendly greeting, warm tone of voice, empathising with how busy she and her boss were, clearly explaining my situation and the pressures, predicting anything she might need to know like how long Bob would be needed for, and above all a warm sense of humour, all these worked miracles.

I then had the task of speedily building those critical deep relationships yet again once I stepped into the executives' offices. Thankful that I had prepared the ground with the PAs, it worked.

Putting the face to the name and the message

My plan was to produce three DVDs for the roadshow. My view was that if I had the executives and senior managers on camera, we would travel the country with them in this way. This would enable them to get their messages across directly to their people, while providing a solution to the challenge of the requirement for them to do so, without them physically being there.

The first two DVDs were of the executive committee members and their senior managers, respectively, revealing their views and key messages to their people with regards to the specific business programme we were working on, which they were responsible for. The third DVD comprised of short highlights of both groups on a DVD which would replay repeatedly in the background at break and lunch times for anyone in the room to absorb whenever they happened to be there.

Enjoying the process

Getting sixteen executives to turn up on the same day to be filmed was a logistical feat. By the time the fourth executive had turned up for his camera interview, word had gone round amongst them that I was a sharp interviewer and wouldn't waste their time. Word also went round that I was a bit of a maverick, "not your normal communication person" and rather fun. So they turned up in force. They could see the point. It saved them time, it helped them manage their programmes and various projects and they enjoyed themselves. Good relationships were enjoyed all round. Job done.

Pulling out the stops for the team

Ordinarily, at this point, it would be usual for an organisation and its communication function to have endless meetings about the cost of producing a DVD or DVDs, tendering out the work, how much it would cost, how many weeks and months it would take and so on and so forth. None of that happened on my watch. I am a highly experienced ex-television reporter, producer and director and was able to use my experience to think fast and think outside the box. I believed in what I was doing and what the division of the organisation (I was working for) was trying to achieve. I thrived on the challenge to get this done and loved the fact that I had a great relationship with a great boss who equally loved what we were achieving together as a team.

There was no time to waste. We needed to make something extraordinary happen fast. I just got on with filming, writing, producing, directing and editing the three DVDs, as part of the service. I called in another good relationship and hired an ex-BBC cameraman who also worked as a one-man band and he did camera and sound. He also had a portable edit suite. Between the two of us, we got the job done quickly and professionally within weeks of my concept. I modestly admit that others would have charged thousands to produce what I produced, taken endless months pontificating with budget sign-offs for expensive sums, especially external agencies, which means it would most likely have never happened, and certainly highly unlikely in the timescales that were demanded. I pulled out the stops, put my back into it, spurred on by the delight in producing something that I believed would build a powerful communication tool and strengthen relationships within the company. The DVDs were made at no extra cost to the company. It got done, and with great pride!

Inspiring everyone to take part

We took the DVDs on the road. My boss headlined the roadshow, with senior managers also on stage. They were there in person to participate in question and answer sessions. We also hired a few professional actors to do some fun role-playing on training and up-skilling specific parts of the business community and what it would take to do that, which formed part of the programme we were working on.

On stage, we also had team members from the business, who were up for acting alongside the real actors in the improvised play. The business participants really got into the spirit of it, and their positive energy was just the tonic for their colleagues watching. It was great fun and went down a storm.

The first roadshow was such a success that by end of it, we had hundreds of impacted colleagues signing up to attend the other dozen roadshows we had lined up around the country. In the end we had over 1000 colleagues, almost the entire business division, turn up to our roadshows. By the end of the second roadshow, word had got to the executive committee members of our success. They then wanted to be part of that success, so a group of them created time in their busy diaries and took it in turns to fly to whichever location we were in and joined us in person. So there we were showing them on DVD with their views and messages of the programme and their personal message to impacted colleagues, and then, they were there in person too, which doubled the credibility ratings of everything the programme was and stood for, for the people.

The end justified the means!

The results were phenomenal. The presence and commitment of the executives, made a huge impact on colleagues and completely transformed their attitude and behaviours, engagement and buy-in of the programme we worked on. This was vital because the programmes success and therefore the business's success depended on them. We cracked it, deep relationships, enthusiastic cooperation and effective communication played a critical role. Magic!

The Innovative Communicator

Building deep relationships – summary

As an Innovative Communicator you will build deep relationships when you:

Make the time and effort to find out who your colleagues are. What makes them tick?

Develop unique bonds with your colleagues.

Really listen to what a colleague has to say.

Use your intuition and perception to spot opportunities, times and places to begin or have conversations that build relationships.

Allow time for a relationship to develop with depth.

Become a confidante people can trust. Operate with diplomacy, discretion, trust and integrity.

Communicate authentically so that your genuine character and behaviour shines through – a highly appealing quality.

Empathise and feel the changes that are required for others.

Build a relationship with the organisational blocker too. Once won over, they will become a great champion to the cause.

Take care not to tread on toes.

Develop the art of effective persuasion.

Inspire others to participate.

Go the extra mile. It reaps rewards.

Questions to think about

- Which parts of the chapter had particular significance for you in terms of the building of deep relationships in the workplace?

- What might you do differently with regard to your relationship with any of the following:

- A single individual in your work place?

- People who work above your level?

- People who work below your level?

- Your employees in general?

Exercise

If you do one thing today: Identify someone in your organisation that you need to build a relationship with and start the process using whichever of the suggestions in this chapter you feel are appropriate.

3

Get your team on board

> *"Every business needs a united team, fully on board, bound by team spirit and determined to achieve collectively. At the heart of this is powerful communication."*
>
> **Miti Ampoma**

The team dilemma

In a well-known, large, British financial organisation, a team member called Jake, explains why he and colleagues are not on board. They are simply not *feeling it*!

Jake sent the following email to a dedicated electronic communication box I set up to get to the truth of a well-known large organisation, where management operated a minimalist to non-existent communication policy in practice, despite their company blurb stating "Communication is one of the top three strategic priorities in our company".

"Hello. Firstly just so this doesn't seem like a whinge, through Project Zebra I have been re-located to Littlepuzzle and now work with a wider variety of people and have a job I hope will give me more experience and better prospects in the long term. I'm therefore fairly happy with the outcome of the project. This is quite a turn around from my initial reaction – after being re-located from Reading to Huddersfield (my home city) and then being told two months later I was being re-located to Littlepuzzle. I was fairly unhappy!

Get your team on board

I do have the following comments:

Personal Experience: Like many, I have been under a lot of stress over the past few months with Project Zebra, the latest finance transformation programme. The Huddersfield team have reduced from five people to just me and my Business As Usual (BAU) workload has doubled. Other projects have led to a lot of questions being thrown at me regarding our modelling. No one has supported or helped me provide the answers to communicate to those who enquire. As I am now the only person in the team, I have had to deal with these queries on top of BAU. I don't feel I know enough about the programme, I feel vital details are being kept hidden, I feel left in the dark and I am keen for more information of what these changes actual mean for me, my colleagues and customers.

In addition to the added pressure my holidays have been affected. I got married two months ago and had to come into work in the middle of my honeymoon to complete month end.

Given the pressure I've had to put up with and the commitment shown, it irritates me that some managers have little appreciation for this and the importance of actually communicating with me at all, let alone on a regular basis. Why is this so difficult? Without any decent communication it makes things even more difficult.

Team experience: As I mentioned I have since moved to Littlepuzzle where I am now part of a wider team. My colleagues are great, but we are all in agreement that we have no idea what is happening. When we first arrived, there was no handover, we just picked up the pieces. But now we don't really get any sense of why we are doing what we are doing daily. What is the purpose of this transformation programme? How is it really going to affect us over the next twelve months? The little information we have so far from management is so high level it's meaningless. I personally think it might not be as bad as others are making out, but because there is a vacuum of any meaningful information of any kind on a regular basis, people are just making things up! Please can someone give us a realistic picture on User Acceptance Testing (UAT) and training? We know the Automation project will affect us, but how? How can we be on board and help when we have no idea of what's going on? Every time we ask we're told information will come, but it's been months now and there's been nothing. The result is the team is feeling disengaged and sceptical and there is a rumour mill building up.

Phil Truck's team is diminishing by the day because those who are left in the team have had far too much work dumped on them and no one communicates with them or tells them anything.

We also appear to be recruiting more people than we have displaced. Why? Can someone explain this to us?

Summary: It seems that there is a real under-appreciation of us at the moment as people, as no one bothers to talk to us, as well as for the amount of work we do and the work we don't have the resource to do. Instead of all of us pulling together there is suspicion, muddle, infighting and confusion. Will someone please talk to us and tell us what is happening? Thank you."

Putting the jigsaw together

Without a strong, united team, bound by team spirit, based on and nurtured by effective people-to-people communication, a team cannot pull together in the same direction to collectively achieve its business goals. The power of transformative communication is dependent on getting people actively involved in the most effective way. So how you get people involved is as important as getting them involved.

> **The key to success is influencing and persuading team members that your goals are worth striving for.**

Do this by keeping them updated and involved in discussions and updates on a consistent and regular basis. Do so in a meaningful way that is relevant to them and their world, rather than a one-off wonder from your point of view which makes little or no difference to them or worse still pays lip-service to the process of communicating with them. Keep your communication honest, punchy, informative, relevant and interesting. Your communication to team members must be easy to understand and make sense. It should get people to see the whole picture of the way your business is moving forward and get them involved.

Getting people involved and on board is like putting together a massive complex jigsaw puzzle with tiny intricate pieces. How you do this is also a delicate juggling act. The diplomacy, discretion and courageous action based on a 'doing' approach is akin to performing the juggling act of walking on eggshells and ensuring you don't crack an egg (because you can't afford to!).

As an Innovative Communicator you are the catalyst for enabling abundant team spirit and for getting team members onside and on-board. You also work as a connector, connecting people to each other, joining up the dots and giving people access to one another in a seamless fashion – just quietly getting it done, so it happens.

Five key things that you're up against when trying to unite a disaffected team:

- Team members have received communication briefings that are too high-level and littered with corporate jargon which leaves them underwhelmed, disengaged and disaffected. To quote a team member "You come out half asleep".

- Team members have received little or no targeted information on what is relevant to them, leaving them frustrated. I've coined this "content free" communication.

- Team members haven't bothered to read monthly messages from leaders because they lack substance and often repeat information communicated before or elsewhere. I've coined this "glaze communication".

- There has been a massive delay in telling team members what is going on, so they found out through leaks, gossip, corridor conversations and rumour mills, leaving them suspicious and resistant to change.

- Team members have not been given bad news honestly – it drives them mad and leaves them angry. They often see through the dishonesty. They would rather know the truth!

The Innovative Communicator's role in getting everyone on board

It is important to adopt a creative approach to any team activities you develop and plan. When it comes to people, creativity at the heart of a business however large or small and whatever its core expertise, is a huge motivator that enables the building of great team spirit and hence great teams. This can be achieved without incurring further costs outside existing allocated budgets.

To get your team on board you need to do team things!

Face2face – a team briefing process to produce emotional benefit

What Jake and his team colleagues desperately needed was to receive the emotional benefits of feeling genuinely valued, recognised for their contribution and hard work, supported, cared for, and to know and feel that they actually mattered. To do this we quickly created (we are talking a few weeks here, not months!) a team briefing process called Face2face which got Jake, his team colleagues and manager talking, exchanging views and ideas, getting to know each other and building long-overdue relationships on a regular monthly basis.

Face2face was set up to support the central and local communication network to meet team needs. The local part of the process was tailored specifically to meet the needs of local teams, like Jake's.

In a two-way direct engagement process, team leaders, who were responsible for front-line staff like Jake and his colleagues, would lead structured team meetings with their managers present, taking part and being part of the conversations. Managers however did not lead the meetings, their team leaders did. This made a significant difference because front-line staff trusted their team leaders in a way they didn't their managers, whom they felt were remote. Relationships with managers therefore needed to be built or rebuilt as quickly as possible, but over appropriate time.

How it worked

Every month the following happened:

- A core brief of relevant company-wide information was produced by Group internal communication. This was based on information from the Group Executives and from stories across the business.

- The group-wide core brief was added to by each division or local function, adding information that was of particular relevance to their specific audience. (I wrote the divisional and local information myself.)

- Managers were given the total brief on a monthly basis, and due to the vacuum in relationships, they would pass on the total brief to their team leaders to manage, carry out and lead a team meeting, (with managers participating) discussing in detail information that was particularly relevant to team members.

- A feedback form was made available for team leaders and staff to feedback questions and comments to either their local communication department or to Group internal communication.

- We would collate and read every feedback form. Questions were answered in the next team meeting or on an individual basis.

The Innovative Communicator

Face2face feedback loop diagram

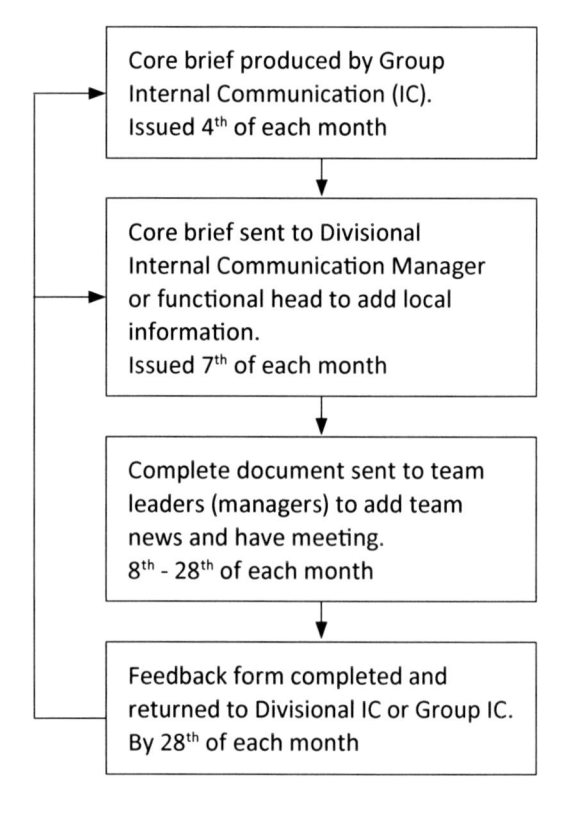

```
┌─────────────────────────────────┐
│ Core brief produced by Group    │
│ Internal Communication (IC).    │
│ Issued 4th of each month        │
└─────────────────────────────────┘
              ↓
┌─────────────────────────────────┐
│ Core brief sent to Divisional   │
│ Internal Communication Manager  │
│ or functional head to add local │
│ information.                    │
│ Issued 7th of each month        │
└─────────────────────────────────┘
              ↓
┌─────────────────────────────────┐
│ Complete document sent to team  │
│ leaders (managers) to add team  │
│ news and have meeting.          │
│ 8th - 28th of each month        │
└─────────────────────────────────┘
              ↓
┌─────────────────────────────────┐
│ Feedback form completed and     │
│ returned to Divisional IC or    │
│ Group IC.                       │
│ By 28th of each month           │
└─────────────────────────────────┘
```

Feedback forms

Our feedback forms had five clear guidelines:

- Which items on the briefing document promoted most interest and discussion?

- Please detail any issues, ideas or suggestions your team members want to raise divisionally, or with the business Executive team.

- Please detail any questions you were unable to answer or topics that you require further information on.

- What subjects, if any, would you like to see covered in future sessions?

- Please detail any other comments you have about Face2face in general.

In the case of Jake's team we held much needed relationship building and moral boosting, Face2face meetings every two weeks for the first two months to kick-start things! By the end of the third month the information flow, understanding, energy and team spirit amongst the team, including their manager had changed completely.

Team Leaders thrived on being empowered with the responsibility of actively owning and running these meetings and they were pivotal to building strong relationships between their front-line staff and managers.

They were given full support and skills training wherever required and requested. They thrived on it! Many became truly Innovative Communicators.

Here is an email communication from Jake's Team leader – we'll call her Milly John to her team of fifty, flagging up the Face2face meeting.

From: Milly John
Sent: 11 March
To: Team members (50 people)

Subject: Face2face team meeting on 20 March

Well I'm planning another fun packed team meeting on 20 March

I have just distributed the Face2face for March and in order to understand all that is going on I would like you all to be involved in this, so the plan is that I would like you in groups to present back one or more of the items on the communication to the rest of the group. Each group will have 15 mins to deliver back:

So I would like:

Jilly, Sally B, Kirsty, Chris H and Susie to present Release 2.2 Go Live Update; Bob C, Mary and Jessica to present CRICK Implementation and CHR; Mike, John, Jane, David and Frank to present IS & Risk & Compliance.

You know as a member of staff what all of us want to know, so I would like you to read through the sections you will be covering and pull out the information that YOU feel is relevant. If you want to include quizzes or anything that can make the learning fun then carry on – it's a chance to deliver the communication in a style that you feel comfortable with.

I would suggest that each group goes away from their desks to discuss how they can carry this out so I have booked time for each group to do this. I will send appointments shortly:

Jilly, Sally B, Kirsty, Chris H and Susie to present Release 2.2 Go Live Update – Wills Room 10-11 on 13/3

Bob C, Mary and Jessica to present CRICK Implementation and CHR – Wills Room 11.30 – 12.30 on 14/3

Mike, John, Jane, David and Frank to present IS & Risk & Compliance – Wills Room 2-3 on 15/3

If you need any help or support give me a shout!

Milly John
Team Leader
Money Purchase Department

Get your team on board

Follow-up email a week later:

From: Milly John
Sent: 18 March
To: Team

Subject: Face2face for March

Hey it's me again!

For March's Face2face, I've attempted to produce a Wordsearch that I will be handing out in my Team Meeting and giving out prizes for the ones who find the most words.

I attach the Wordsearch if you're interested in using it.

I've got the answers in paper format if you want to come and get a copy – you might even want to attempt it yourself!

I've also put together a short fun quiz to get us all going!

Adrian and Martha – Please circulate this email if you feel your Team Leaders may be interested in using it.

Cheers
Milly John
Team Leader
Money Purchase Department

The Innovative Communicator

Milly's Wordsearch

Wordsearch

In the Wordsearch below, there are 11 abbreviations that are mentioned in February's Face2face communication:

TROT	A document management system for procedure notes
AMS	Agency Management Scheme
SSP	Shared Services Programme
GT	Group Technology
FSA	Financial Services Act
WAKE	A new workflow tool to enable effective work management
IS	Information Systems
AE	Agent Earnings
CIS	Customer Illustration System
EBS	Employee Benefit Solutions
DMS	Document Management Services

T	R	O	T	E	I	A	M	S	H
E	C	B	O	Q	E	O	D	Y	S
G	T	X	J	B	M	F	S	P	S
I	P	F	Z	U	A	I	T	I	P
O	S	R	C	L	S	W	C	S	R
A	U	J	G	K	X	Q	E	J	O
Z	P	W	A	K	E	T	R	A	E
X	A	S	H	D	R	F	U	I	L
W	M	J	S	L	S	P	L	D	F
D	A	V	B	Y	F	E	C	B	H
N	T	S	E	C	W	I	X	L	Y
P	B	Z	X	B	U	G	K	E	A

Get your team on board

Milly's Quiz questions

The answers are supplied here. Milly supplied them separately.

Risk Compliance

1. What are the three main steps to money laundering?
   Answer: Placement, layering, integration.

2. What is the Operational Risks main function?
   Answer: To ensure everyone is trained e.g. Team Leaders.

5. What is the main function of the Compliance team?
   Answer: To make sure systems and work meet industry regulations.

IS Support

1. Name the three functions of the ISS team?
   Answer: Applications support, service delivery, technical delivery.

2. Name the main purpose of the ISS team?
   Answer: To make sure Automated Solutions and User Acceptance Testing are fit for purpose and meet strict new regulatory standards.

3. When was the new ISS team put in place?
   Answer: February.

The Innovative Communicator

Team Leader Milly John's local Face2face meeting agenda outline:

Agenda

The Face2face communication meeting:
20 March 2009 in RDG G Meeting Room 2, BHO, 3pm.

- Presentations from February's Face2face communication.

- Release 2.2. Go Live Update – Jilly, Sally B, Kirsty, Chris H and Susie.

- Crick Implementation & CHR – Bob C, Mary and Jessica.

- IS & Risk Compliance – Mike, John, Jane, David and Frank.

- Team discussion and questions following the briefing.

- Wordsearch and Fun Quiz.

- Feedback from last month's questions raised.

- Any other business (AOB).

Face2face was a briefing concept that was rolled across the business and refined to suit the company business-wide. Although there were already many valuable team meetings occurring within the business at various levels, this wasn't the case in all parts of the business. The Face2face system ensured that this happened company wide, that all staff received regular, consistent information about the company and most importantly, that a more formal process of feedback from staff to management was established. The whole process was driven by and focussed on getting teams on board and doing it really well, so that the tangible benefits were evident for the business.

The bottom line was that communication was targeted appropriately. There was awareness of business-wide group information, a more detailed update of divisional or functional news, and equally important was local information specifically relevant and tailored to local teams. This clear communication tripartite changed the dynamics and got teams on board. It made sense to them because they could see and feel the benefits of the communication.

Persuading a reluctant director

Toby Courage is one of the directors in Jake's company. He is reluctant to give the time to communication activities which will take people away from their desks for the sake of emotional benefit. The key issue is to persuade directors like Toby that just because it isn't immediately scientifically quantifiable, putting a focus on "human emotional benefit" produces sustainable, successful, human relationships and will result in happy staff, happy customers and great profits. By giving emotional benefit dedicated time, we are putting the soul back into business. We are making the "soul" quantifiable.

My job was to persuade Toby that allowing time to achieve emotional benefit would give him exactly the successful results he wanted to achieve.

Toby: Hello Miti, come in. Sorry to have kept you waiting. How are you?

Miti: I'm very well Toby. Many thanks for your time. I know how busy you are, so it's much appreciated.

Toby: What can I do for you?

Miti: *[With a warm smile]*
I'm hoping to persuade you to the merits of having a new communication vehicle dedicated specifically to ensuring that your team remains fully on board with the programme's goals. I come pre-warned, that you might be hard to persuade. Toby, I know you'll agree that this programme is humungous with huge implications not just for the business but obviously for the country, so I think it's imperative that we have some appropriate team specific communication to make sure the team is fully engaged, on board and heading in the same direction. At present there is nothing to keep them together. Your team in just four months has grown from under a dozen people in one office to almost one hundred spread across the

country. In the next couple of months that number is set to grow. I'm concerned that due to the geographical spread and the pressure they are under, there's a danger of them becoming a disparate force rather than a force to be reckoned with, collectively driving through these changes and singing from the same hymn sheet so to speak. What do you think?

Toby: [Smiles warmly back]
Hmmm, I see what you're saying, but my issue is the very point you make, they are under pressure because there's a lot of work to do and I need them to get the work done. I don't want them distracted by taking that time away from them. Don't they talk regularly on conference calls and dial-ins? Why won't that do? You're right, I'm afraid I will need to be convinced and I'm not convinced as yet that the benefits outweigh what I need getting done.

Miti: I was going to suggest that we invite them for a regular monthly face to face meeting, led by your Programme Manager, Sam Long, and you, if you wanted. I think we should call it Team Talk! It would be a forum which would give team members the opportunity to hear directly from you both. You in turn can hear from them directly and get to know them, Toby. I think that's important. Your presence will give visibility and credibility to the notion of senior management's commitment for these changes. Given your understandable concerns about the time pressures, how about we say everyone meets once every six to eight weeks rather than once a month?

Toby: Well I do like the title Team Talk and there is definitely merit in the opportunity for team members and I to interact in the way you describe. Tell you what, can you write me a paper on this? Just a one pager will do. Something I can quickly read and I'll come back to you.

Miti: Of course, no problem. When would you like it?

Toby: Can you get it to me within the next couple of days?

Get your team on board

Miti: Absolutely consider it done. Can I ask, when might you be able to fully consider the proposal and come back to me?

Toby: *[Smiling broadly]*
There's no let up with you on deadlines and definitives is there Miti? OK I'll give you a "Yes" or "No" by the end of next week.

Miti: *[Broad grin]*
That'll be brilliant. Thank you, thank you, thank you. You are the best! I could hug you. I promise it'll really enhance team performance if you were to give permission to go ahead. I won't let you down.

Toby: *[Laughs]*
I'll give it serious consideration Miti. I'll look forward to the one-pager.

Miti: Thanks again Toby. I really appreciate it.

Forty-eight hours later I handed a Team Talk one-page proposal to Toby. Within a week he gave us the go-ahead to start Team Talk, the first of its kind in the organisation.

Warmth, humour and clear honesty enabled me to begin to get Toby's cooperation, and delivering my promise secured it. Toby was vital in his role as a company director, and it was critical that I got him on board.

The Team Talk forum proposal

The Team Talk proposal was a regular monthly face-to-face meeting of the entire Programme team including horizontal reports – led by Toby Courage and Sam Long. This is what the proposal looked like:

Duration: 1 hour
How often: every 6-8 weeks
Led by: Sam Long and Toby Courage
Starts when: Thursday: 5th March
Location: Pride Street, London
Organised by: Miti Ampoma – Programme Communication Manager

Purpose:

Once every 6-8 weeks, Team Talk (team meetings) will take place involving the entire Programme team including horizontal reports and project managers across the business. All team members are strongly encouraged to attend in person. There are no dial-ins. This is a face-to-face gathering providing the opportunity for the entire programme team to hear directly from Sam and Toby. The agenda will be structured, interactive, relaxed and informal, with the opportunity for lots of questions and answers between team members and Sam and Toby.

Why the need?

- Regular consistent 6-8 weekly face to face meetings keeps team members informed and updated of the programme, latest business and relevant parent Group events, associated programmes, particularly developments that impact and/or affect our programme and/or the context in which our programme sits in the wider extensive change programme of the business

- The programme team now has almost 100 people spread in various locations across the business. This is the only opportunity for the whole team to meet and come together

Get your team on board

- Relationship rapport building and networking between team members

- Knowledge exchange and sharing of ideas between team members

- Information for team members about our specific programme and the wider programme gained directly from Sam and Toby (face to face)

- Senior management are seen to be visibly supporting colleagues in their efforts, demonstrating their support for and commitment to the programme. It will also raise the profile of the programme as guest speakers including other relevant stakeholders are invited to give updates and/or their perspectives over topics of the day, progress and challenges

- The one hour meeting will be scheduled so it is followed by informal socialising afterwards

The Innovative Communicator's role as the vital connector for others

Having got everyone on board through a carefully planned briefing process, the Innovative Communicator's role is to keep the team working together, keep them enthusiastic and keep them fully engaged.

Team Talk – a communication forum that connects directors and their teams

The first two Team Talks went very well. I managed to get the Chief Information Officer (CIO) of the company to be our guest speaker and this was a huge success. By the third Team Talk we were on a roll and it had become a must attend event for Team members. On this occasion, against the odds, I managed to get the Chief Operating Officer (COO) to be our guest speaker.

Team Talk was always scheduled for 4pm for one hour, followed immediately by informal networking and socialising. Our guest speakers would always join us for this and so got to know our programme team members individually, and through them became a lot closer to the detail of our programme than they would otherwise have had the opportunity to do. They bonded with the team and built relationships with them. This was great for team morale, great for work, great for the programme and great for the business. Everyone was fully on board voluntarily, keen to contribute to the success of the goals.

The format was that Sam and Toby would introduce Team Talk. Our guest speaker would then speak for fifteen to twenty minutes and the remaining thirty-five to forty minutes would be taken up with discussion, questions and answers. As part of the planning, I always booked a nearby venue for an after work drink followed by an optional evening meal, which were self-funding. We had 100 % take up. It was widely acknowledged that more business issues, problem solving and immediate follow-up meetings, were concluded over the drinks and evening meals face-to-face in one evening than many normally achieved in a week's work at the office.

Team Talk created the access for people in business to connect with each other, network, build relationships and get to know each other better. It also gave them access to meet, listen to and personally get to know some of the most senior executive sponsors of their work on a first hand basis – something that would not have happened without Team Talk. The programme went on to be named as a Best Transformational Improvement Award finalist – out of almost 2000 nominations – in a prestigious Group plc awards scheme. One of the notable recognitions from the executives and award judges for the programmes accolade was how fully on board the programme team members were and the role they played in delivering a highly successful programme for the business. Communication was recognised as central to this success.

The input necessary for getting your team on board is on-going, focussed hard work that requires sharp intuition and an instinct for an audience. The output and results are stunning and transforms companies and businesses. It is worth pursuing.

Getting your team involved and on board – summary

Getting your team on board is pivotal to your success. Without them you will struggle to reach your goals.

Avoid letting process and technology override the human spirit. Process and technology should support not hinder.

Be creative in your communication strategy and approach to winning hearts and minds.

If you seriously want to win hearts and minds do not "cascade" information via technology alone. Get human beings to work with your teams face-to-face using the information you want to share to influence and persuade. Cascading is often used as a "get out" clause for not communicating difficult messages, often ending in Chinese whispers, misinterpretation and misunderstanding.

If you find yourself saying "Communication is one our top three strategic business priorities" *or* "We are all in this together", make sure you mean it and will back it up with visible action. Otherwise it'll rile your team and turn them off in droves!

Work quickly to provide communication solutions and action them.

Strike a balance between healthy collaborative discussion and endless inconclusive meetings, so you can take decisions and go do!

Build in enjoyable activities for people, such as quizzes, social get-togethers, and appropriate situations where they can generally feel valued and free to say what they need to say while having fun. The by-product is that much work gets done and many problems are solved.

Questions to think about

- If you are experiencing change in your organisation, who are the teams you might need to get involved in communicating those changes?

- Which team leaders, managers or executives might you start by supporting?

- How might you communicate your message most directly to relevant team leaders, managers or executives?

- What kind of structure for communicating with your team leaders, managers or executives might you set up?

- What kind of enjoyable activities might help to support your communication plan?

- How might you effectively organise the follow-up to feedback requests you receive?

Exercise

If you do one thing today take a face-to-face team boosting *mood-ometer* at your next meeting. Gather and discuss the top five ideas with your people on what they would specifically like to see happen to further build team spirit and morale. Implement the best ideas with majority agreement.

4

Build your strategy

> *"If you want your staff to understand your goals and work as a team to provide solutions, you need communication between people to drive performance. If you really want to drive performance, then you need clear, bold, effective communication and that always requires a strategy."*
> **Miti Ampoma**

A classic company dilemma

After an extensive year-long search a major British company with a long-established history and rich heritage, agreed to enter into exclusive discussions with a leading international consultancy with the aim of setting up a joint venture. This joint venture would create a new company that would take over third-party administration services within the British company. 1200 people from the British company would be transferred as employees to the international company, leaving just 200 staff in the British company. We'll call the British company Blue Sky and the International company Far Seas.

Far Seas was a provider of IT consulting services, systems integration and Business Process Outsourcing (BPO) operations. The problem was that despite a few updates to the Blue Sky employees relating to the possibility of BPO, the reality was clear:

- A BPO project in Blue Sky lacked visibility and identity.

- BPO was not being recognised by the majority of Blue Sky staff.

- BPO was a complex process which needed clear explanation and understanding.

- BPO was closely associated with off shore outsourcing, so most staff believed it was "all about job cuts and the dread of losing their jobs". The rumour mill was rife, morale low, and productivity at risk.

With a joint venture partnership agreement between Blue Sky and Far Seas imminent, Blue Sky needed to build an internal and external communication strategy and execute it as soon as possible. Further more, with Far Seas investing almost £500 million over ten years in the strategic partnership, they were in practice the dominant partner in this joint venture. That too needed appropriate positioning with Blue Sky staff. We'll shortly look in detail at the communication strategy that Blue Sky implemented.

Why you need to build a strategy

As businesses get bigger or more complex in structure, I've consistently found that the more people you've got, the higher likelihood you'll have communication problems that impact your bottom line.

Your people are dealing with lots of change, pressure to perform, business goals and targets they need to understand and meet, and the mistake is that you assume they understand what you want.

That's not what happens.

There are unnecessary delays and highly expensive recurring mistakes that just don't seem to resolve. Problems typically show up as unhappy customers and disgruntled employees with their arms folded, rumour mills, corridor conversations and no buy-in.

So, ultimately, the proof is that the required performance just isn't there – and the bigger your organisation, the more likelihood of these problems.

You want your people to understand your goals and work as a team to provide solution, don't you? To do this you need communication between people to drive performance. If you really want to drive performance, then you need clear, bold, effective communication, and that *always* requires a strategy.

Blue Sky communication strategy – a case study

Below I've set out full details of the Blue Sky communication strategy and plan, to enable you to adapt elements of it to your own business. It is followed by general tips and advice for strategy building.

Every strategy needs four key phases:

- Scoping
- Design
- Roll out
- Review

The following case study illustrates these phases.

The Internal Communication Strategy – to address staff

SCOPING

My first job after building deep relationships, building trust, gathering information, understanding the issues and collaborating with others, was to put together and agree with the relevant people the key priorities for an effective communication programme.

Agreed priorities:

- To continue to emphasise that it was business as normal – the joint venture was an opportunity for growth not job cuts.

- To create an identity and brand for BPO and Blue Sky, called the core organisation during the transition period.

- To keep all staff up-to-date with developments regularly and consistently.

- To vary the communication media to drive key messages.

- To work out a set of *key messages* which would be central to the communication plan.

- To enable depth of understanding by staff of what was happening, when, where and by whom.

- To achieve clarity and simplicity in all communication.

Key Messages

Key messages are one of the fundamental building blocks of building a good strategy and they need to be created after detailed discussions, interviews, formal conversations and informal chats with all those who are relevant to the programme, project or business goals.

I came up with the following key messages for the internal communication strategy:

- Far Seas is bringing its globally recognised expertise and skills to our UK industry. The company is now in talks with us with the aim of setting up a new company based here in Blue Valley.

- The new company will continue to be based in Blue Valley where Blue Sky staff currently work, enabling a seamless transition and the continuation of business as normal.

- This multimillion pound investment (£500 million over the next ten years) by Far Seas based in Blue Valley, will help create a powerful new centre of excellence in our market.

- The new company will provide fresh job opportunities, on-going career development and long-term job security for employees.

- Current staff are key to the success of the new company. The success of the proposed business plans depends on the existing Blue Sky staff. Far Seas cannot succeed without us. We are in this together.

- The new company will specialise in third party administration services for our particular business. Further future business will be

Build your strategy

generated by sales of Business Process Outsourcing (BPO) to other companies.

- The new Blue Valley based company will become a leader in its field by combining Blue Sky's industry experience, strength and knowledge with Far Seas input, investment and global track record.

- The new company will give our customers greater value and enable us to provide them with an even higher standard of service.

Key Audiences

There are two categories of key audiences:

1. People you need to get on board to build the strategy by developing deep relationships and getting them involved.

2. People you are going to inform about the strategy once you've built it.

Having successfully developed deep relationships to work with the right people as a team, we clearly identified those we needed to inform. In this case there were three main audiences:

- The Commercial division of the business
- Staff Transferring to Far Seas
- Staff staying at Blue Sky

For each of these audiences we needed to map out the messages that were relevant and specific to them.

Key messages – Commercial division
- It's business as normal, comfort, reassure, motivate
- We are creating a Centre of Excellence, win-win benefits
- Bringing new business to Blue Valley
- No offshoring of jobs
- Major IT investment
- Blue Sky leading transfer to Far Seas
- Seamless business transfer
- Far Seas establishing a UK subsidiary of huge parent group Light Seas
- Far Seas attributes size, financial strength and expertise
- Far Seas building a business in Blue Valley
- IT infrastructure investment
- Transfer date early 2007
- End of July confirmation details of transferring and retained structure

Key Messages – Staff transferring
- Jobs remain in Blue Valley
- Creation of a Centre of Excellence in our field
- Growth business in Blue Valley
- Good career opportunities
- Transfer of Terms and Conditions
- Transfer of majority of HR policies and procedures
- Pension contributions intention to be matched by Far Seas
- Acceptance of current culture
- Comprehensive Consultation Process

Key messages – staff staying
- Focus on our core business
- Growth of business in Blue Valley
- Highly specialised and breadth of roles
- Management of finance, governance and suppliers
- Acquisition of closed book of business
- Good Career opportunities
- Comprehensive Consultation Process
- No change to terms and conditions
- No change to pension arrangements

Build your strategy

Vehicles of communication

Drawing on experience from other outsourcing projects within Blue Sky as well as extensive research, I drew up a list of the most effective ways to develop Blue Sky staff (both senior managements' and workers') awareness, develop their understanding and gain their buy-in and ownership of BPO. These were some of the proven channels:

- Staff group briefings
- Team Briefings
- Consultation Process
- Communication Meetings with Far Seas
- Round table engagement
- Formal and informal staff consultation meetings
- Staff newsletters
- Staff survey
- Trade Union consultation
- Questions and answers
- Pension workshops

We then added the following to the communication vehicle list:

- Set up a specific Far Seas Information Centre
- Set up Far Seas Presentations
- Set up a joint Far Seas and Blue Sky Exhibition Stand with material to reflect the new company
- Organise a launch event
- Consultation with Trade Unions

The following *external* vehicles were added to the internal vehicles listed above:

- Media contact, local and national
- Third party contracts (for example suppliers)
- Customer Contact
- Blue Sky's regulating body
- Inland Revenue
- Key contacts (for example banks)
- Local government contact

Communication Strategy – detailed method

Internal vehicles of communication – staff

STAFF GROUP BRIEFINGS
Objective
To ensure that all staff are briefed at a strategic level with key messages.

Output
Clarity, consistency and continuity of the key messages.

Group staff briefings led by the Director of the Commercial Division, will take place in September and bi-monthly going forward. The briefings will be at a strategic level and the aim will be to deliver where possible just two key messages: firstly the update on the business and secondly developments relating to Business Process Outsourcing (BPO). This will help to focus direct attention on BPO and link the priority of achieving a seamless transfer without impacting on service delivery

TEAM BRIEFINGS
Objective
To ensure that all staff have the opportunity to discuss the key messages in more detail and the relevance to that business area and what it will mean in practice.

Output
Understanding the detail of the key messages.

All Line Managers will be responsible for briefing their staff following Group Presentations and when required, for both the retained and transferring staff. They will be closely supported by Communication Specialists and the HR team, and comprehensive briefings notes will be produced to ensure that there is clarity and consistency in the messages to staff. Feedback and all questions and answers from service meetings will be collaged. Where Managers are unable to answer questions, there will be a commitment to go back to the staff member with an answer within five working days.

Build your strategy

COMMUNICATION MEETINGS
Objective
To ensure that the internal and external communications between Blue Sky, Mediaplus (our external communication agency support), Far Seas and third parties are managed appropriately.

Output
Total understanding of the differing agendas and priorities. Accurate and timely delivery of all communication.

A minimum of fortnightly communication meetings with all representatives. A prime role of these meetings will be to agree and plan communication activity and check progress against planned targets.

STAFF CONSULTATION
Objective
To achieve clarity and simplicity in the consultation and communication process and to ensure depth, full reach and understanding of communication.

Output
Business as normal and to meet the HR TUPE legislative requirements relating to consultation and communication.

FORMAL STAFF CONSULTATION MEETINGS
It is proposed that Line Managers hold individual meetings in October and January with transferring staff to deal with any individual issues and concerns, which may not have been addressed by the other methods of communication. We will provide briefings for all Line Managers and they will refer to Communication and HR if they are unable to answer questions.

There will be a commitment to answer questions and queries within five working days. We will have appointment sessions for people to pre-book on either an individual basis, or (recognising that some employees may find this a little daunting) we will also offer the opportunity for them to bring a colleague with them. We will raise staff awareness of these sessions through newsletters, notice board material and our intranet.

STAFF NEWSLETTER
Starting in October, we will produce newsletters every two weeks for all employees to keep them informed of the developments on the new organisation. This will include business update, timescales and information on the Trade Union meetings. Joint newsletters with Far Seas will be considered at the earliest practical opportunity. The first newsletter will

notify employees of the start of the formal consultation period. This will also include details of the TUPE appeals process and will also inform them of the Trade Union Elected Representatives.

STAFF LETTERS
The first letter will be sent in February after the contract is signed – anticipating a transfer date as early as possible in 2007. The final letter will be sent the day of the transfer giving notification of change of employer to Far Seas.

EMPLOYEE PACK
Evidence indicates that people like to have formal information to take away and read with their colleagues and families. We will produce two booklets, one for those who will transfer under TUPE to Far Seas, and a separate one for staff who are staying with Blue Sky. We will also supply a printed folder to enable employees to hold all information in one place. From previous experience we know that staff often keep printed communication material throughout the process and it provides critical information and assurance to them personally.

FAR SEAS STAFF PRESENTATIONS
At the earliest opportunity transferring staff will want to meet the new management team from Far Seas face-to-face, and learn more about the company – especially their approach to pensions, terms and conditions, salary and bonus payments.

FAR SEAS INFORMATION CENTRE
Objective
To increase the visibility of Far Seas and to give employees the opportunity to understand the company in an informal environment

Output
Staff are keen to find out about Far Seas and the information centre is well attended.

We believe that there would be significant benefit in establishing a Far Seas information centre in a meeting room on the ground floor. Far Seas have indicated that they are keen to establish an information centre. The aim of this would be to provide information relating specifically to the Far Seas company and its wider parent group.

The information centre would give staff the opportunity to find out more about the new joint venture contract, understand the Far Seas approach to

Build your strategy

people and meet colleagues from Far Seas. Opening hours/days would need to be discussed and agreed with Far Seas.

PENSION WORKSHOPS
Objective
To give staff the opportunity to attend pension workshops.

Output
Staff have full understanding of both the Blue Sky and Far Seas pension arrangements.

Pension workshops will help to eliminate concern and worry that many staff have when transferring to a new organisation. It would be beneficial to have pension experts from both Blue Sky and Far Seas at the workshops. Timing would be dependent on Far Seas resources.

EXHIBITION STAND MATERIAL
Objective
To increase the profile and visibility of all communication.

Output
An accessible, focal point for all communication material.

We will purchase an exhibition stand on which all communication material will be displayed. The stand will then be located in a prominent position within the ground floor atrium area. Tight control will be maintained on the quality and appearance of the material.

LAUNCH EVENT
Objective
To celebrate the start of the new Far Seas Organisation.

Output
Transferred staff start to feel part of a new organisation. Publicity for the new organization.

Far Seas will organise a launch event on "day one". With a strong emphasis on "welcome", the aim would be to further market and promote the opportunities presented by the new organisation. This would include separate events for staff, press and media, MPs and relevant third parties.

TRADE UNION MEETINGS
Objective
Continue to maintain a robust relationship with our trade union Razorsharp.

Output
Two way communication across the business is achieved.

Razorsharp is the recognised consultative body for the Blue Sky group and they have representation across the total business. We will use this group for two way consultation and communication. A minimum of monthly formal meetings with Trade Unions will be established from October.

External vehicles of communication

MEDIA CONTACT
Our communication expert will liaise and work closely with Mediaplus to ensure weekly communication and joint agreement to all press releases.

THIRD PARTY AND CUSTOMER CONTACT
Letters to third parties and customers will highlight the exciting new venture, and the message that business carries on as normal and there is no impact on the existing relationship. Letters will be sent to all groups lists over the week commencing 15 September.
All Suppliers
Razorsharp
Local MPs
Blue Valley Council Chief Executive
Inland Revenue
Our governing body

A letter will be sent to all customers nearer to the transfer date.

Measurement of Success

Fundamental to the success of a strong innovative communication strategy and its implementation is the process of measuring, monitoring, adjusting and adapting it throughout the life of the programme or project.

Build your strategy

In this case measurement included verbally asking people what they thought of the communication through to a bespoke employee survey about the communication and consultation process, repeated within three months. These techniques proved successful in providing immediate and direct feedback which was then acted on.

Risks and Issues

With an outsourcing goal and programme of this scale, there are risks and issues that need to be recognised and pro-actively managed to minimise any misunderstandings, inappropriate expectations or negative impact, whilst raising its profile and understanding. It's important when building a strategy to be clear about potential risks and issues. Prepare and have actions in place to mitigate potential pitfalls.

Here are some examples of the risks and issues we predicted for Blue Sky.

Risk/Issue	Action
• Information is leaked before the formal agreed presentation • A third party leaks and informs Far Seas before internal Blue Sky plans are finalized	Prepare email to all employees Prepare content in advance but arrange group presentation at short notice Brief Management team. Prepare media release Prepare contingency plan
Risk/Issue	**Action**
• Perceived as redundancy situation	Key message in communications and all presentations
• Perceived negatively by staff	Frequent positive but honest communication
• Scale is misunderstood	Communicate scale at the earlier opportunity and emphasise the reality
• Omitting retained staff	Include in communication plan
• Impact on culture	Presentations from Far Seas to acknowledge and underline commitment to current culture within Blue Sky
• Pension concerns	Pension workshops

DESIGN

Having defined the scope, we began fine tuning the design of the strategy. These were the next steps:

- Agree communication plan with the Leadership Management Team and Far Seas
- Identify personnel to be involved in the development and delivery of the communication programme – internally and from the outsource company
- Define responsibilities
- Agree contact arrangements, protocol and review procedures
- Develop detailed content for each element of communication
- Identify and agree budgets
- Implement!

From this comprehensive strategic thought process with collaboration and agreement, we built the most appropriate strategy. I then wrote up the details and in addition I produced a full action plan to deliver that strategy, which spelt out the *who*, the *what*, the *why*, the *when* and the *where*, as well as, a communication activity timetable of weekly tasks. Finally attached to the weekly activity timetable was an appendix of the communications schedule showing the timeline for implementing the entire communication programme schedule.

We also prepared a holding statement in the form of a written message for internal staff from the Director of the Commercial Division confirming the name of Far Seas as the new strategic partner, what this meant for the business and the next steps, in case that information was leaked to Far Seas before our official launch event to make the announcement. It was important to have this holding statement ready amid the rumours actively circulating. It is vital to be prepared for the "just in case" scenario and to always have a robust plan B. Fortunately however, there was no leak and our launch event announcing the joint venture went ahead, and was a great success.

Build your strategy

Sample of the communication activity weekly task plan
12-19 September

Week 1: 12 – 19 September				
Date	Task/Objective	Lead responsibility	Comments	Completed
Mon 12	Meet with Leadership Team to Discuss comments from Communication Plan, branding and key messages for presentation 18 September	Miti Ampoma Jack Smith		Completed
	Prepare third party letters, ready to send 18 September	Jill Smith Phil Smith		Completed
	Mediaplus to produce contingency media release	Mediaplus Miti Ampoma		Completed
	Inform catering company re lunch arrangements	Jill Smith		Completed
	Inform Far Seas of change to group presentation date	Steven Hope (Group Director)		Completed
Tue 11	Meet with Leadership Team to discuss comments from Communication plan, branding and key messages for 18 September	Miti Ampoma Jack Smith		Completed
	Complete key messages	Miti Ampoma Jack Smith		Completed

Date	Task/Objective	Lead responsibility	Comments	Completed
	Communication meeting with Far Seas	Miti Ampoma Jack Smith	Meeting Wednesday and Thursday	Completed
	Discuss Shareholder questions	Miti Ampoma Jack Smith		Completed
Wed 12	Complete presentation for 18 September	Wendy Hill Jill Smith		Completed
Thur 13	Leadership Team to agree communication activity for next 4 weeks	Leadership Team Miti Ampoma Jack Smith		Completed
	Leadership Team to agree identity	Leadership Team	Commercial agreed	Completed
	Round Table meeting details to be confirmed	Leadership Team Miti Ampoma		Completed
	Blue Sky holding statement to be signed off	Joint Steering Meeting		Completed
	Far Seas to prepare press statement and key messages to share with Blue Sky	Chris Clear		Completed
Fri 14	Complete Questions and Answers internal, external and customers	Mediaplus Miti Ampoma Jack Smith		Completed
	Check Razorsharp (trade union) representatives by business area	Jill Smith		Completed

Build your strategy

Questions and answers

We produced a detailed Questions and Answers document pack to give as much detailed information as was possible at the time, to any questions that might be asked by staff. The quality and usefulness of the document was heavily influenced by the strong relationships made and built with staff at all levels across the business. It gave depth to the quality of the output by making it relevant and vital as a communication tool for understanding, engagement and buy-in.

Examples of the questions included:

- What is happening?
- Who are Far Seas Consultancy Services?
- What is Far Seas Consultancy Services experience in our industry?
- Why have Far Seas Consultancy Services as a strategic long-term partner?
- What will happen to the existing Blue Valley office?
- What is Business Process Outsourcing?

An example of an answer:

> **What is Business Process Outsourcing?**
> As this question was absolutely critical to people's understanding and engagement of the proposed changes, it was important to be very clear. No wooliness, no vagueness. Meaningless warm words for an explanation won't cut it!
>
> **Answer**
> Business Process Outsourcing (BPO) is the contracting of a specific business task, such as payroll, to a third-party service provider. Usually, BPO is implemented as a cost-saving measure for tasks that a company requires, but does not depend upon to maintain their position in the marketplace.
>
> BPO is often divided into two categories: back office *outsourcing* which includes internal business functions such a billing or purchasing, and front office outsourcing which includes customer-related services such as marketing or technical support.

> BPO that is contracted outside a company's own country is sometimes called *offshore outsourcing*.
>
> BPO that is contracted to a company's neighbouring country is sometimes called *nearshore outsourcing* and BPO that is contracted with the company's own country is sometimes called *onshore outsourcing*.
>
> Far Seas will be engaging in an onshore outsourcing operation as Blue Sky's strategic partner. No jobs will be leaving the country and no one will be losing their jobs.

External Communication Strategy and Plan to address the media

An external communication strategy and plan needs to be closely aligned with the internal communication plan.

Here's what we did for Far Seas:

Objectives

- Organise significant global coverage, particularly in the UK and Far East, national, business, wires and specialist trade media

- That coverage contains key messaging that successfully positions and gives context to Far Seas' forthcoming investment in the new company

- Position Far Seas as a new leader in the industry market and differentiate from the competition

- Ensure the announcement has a global and local context to resonate successfully in all markets and with staff of both Far Seas and Blue Sky

- Positive coverage that highlights Far Seas' commitment to UK investment, particularly Blue Valley as a Centre of Excellence

Build your strategy

Strategy

- Proactive strategy from Far Seas, reactive strategy from Blue Sky

- Messaging and execution that is tailored to the individual needs of the global media and specific markets to educate and ensure correct positioning across all coverage and generate positive messages

- Messaging and positioning that puts the announcement in the context of the UK and industry market, the benefits to customers and employees

- Media roll-out that leverages key spokesperson on the first day of the announcement, but continues to reinforce the story going forward until contract closure and beyond

- Use third-party analyst or expert to endorse the joint venture strategy and put it in market context, especially important if Blue Sky is not going to be proactively involved in the news generation on the day

- Use the announcement to continue to differentiate Far Seas from its competitors

Proposed contingency plan

It is vital to have prepared a contingency plan in your external communication that anticipates potential risks and issues, in case things go wrong. This is what we did:

First Warning	
Information appears in the public domain or Media monitoring picks up information or Blue Sky/Far Seas/Mediaplus are called up by a journalist	
Internal Response	**External Response**
1. Joint communication team made aware of situation via email alert - Immediate conference call is scheduled	Reactive press activity by Mediaplus using Q & As and holding statement - All calls forwarded to Mediaplus
2. Joint communication conference call - Assess scale and agree recommendations to be put to Blue Sky/Far Seas management	If agreed, Mediaplus to issue press release to local Blue Valley media
3. Recommendations sent to Far Seas/Mike Black & Steven Hope/Blue Sky team	Far Seas to inform Far East Stock Exchange of intention
4. Communication team uses agreed Q&A document and holding statement in all communication from now on	Far Seas to send out and follow up press release to Far Seas media targets via Mediaplus
5. Decision made to inform Blue Sky staff - Contingency email to be sent to Blue Sky staff - Staff meeting scheduled (Far Seas personnel to attend)	Far Seas to set up one-to-one briefings with Far Seas media targets via Mediaplus
6. Email notification to Blue Sky staff of staff meeting	

Build your strategy

Materials

- Press release
- Q &A
- Backgrounder on Far Seas and Blue Sky
- Good photography
- Up to date biographies for key spokespeople

Key Questions

- Confirm Blue Sky will be handling local media
- Confirm Blue Sky will only be issuing a reactive statement
- Who will be the spokesperson beside Soz? Will we get Mr Kodbab in time?
- Can we engage an analyst/market influencer to endorse announcement?
- Are the analysts being briefed on this announcement?
- With regards content we need to be clear on:
    - How does this announcement impact the UK and Global industry market?
    - Can we talk about the size of Far Seas' potential investment?
    - Why is Far Seas doing this? How does this change the game?
    - What are the benefits for staff?
    - What are the benefits for customers?
    - What are the benefits for UK? Far East country?
    - What are the long/short term benefits to Far Seas?
    - What will the impact be on UK jobs? Far East market?

Next Steps

- Finalise and agree messaging, positioning and context of the announcement
- Draft, finalise and agree Far Seas press release
- Prepare briefing books
- Arrange practice sessions/media refreshers
- Pitch in interviews to media

Critical success factors

- That the announcement is made within the context of the market place
    - Ensure we answer the question, why is Far Seas doing this? How does it change the game?
    - Ensure we have very strong messaging around job creation in the UK
    - Ensure we can address what the announcement means for customers
    - Ensure we can articulate the short and long term benefits to Far Seas
- A core group of spokespeople are available for comment
- Engage a third-party spokesperson to validate the announcement as a trend in the industry

Execution

- Global press release issued by Far Seas, reactive statement available from Blue Sky
- The news must be delivered within the context of the ramifications for the UK and global industry market
- Global media roll-out tailored for individual markets
    - UK Series of one-on-one briefings and telephone briefings for Tier 1 press, conference for Tier 2 and trade
    - Suggest *Financial Times* as key media source
    - Blue Sky to handle local media
    - Far East: In-country press conference
    - Global: Telephone briefings with Tier 1 media
- The announcement roll-out has to fit with the opening times of the International Stock Exchange (ISE) and also occur in parallel or post the announcement being made to Blue Sky employees, with this in mind please see proposed interview timetable
- Agree key spokespeople that are available on the day and following the announcement for interview
    - Suggest Soz, Mr Kodbab (Global Chief Executive) conduct Tier 1 interviews
    - Sihabi and Mike to conduct Tier 2 UK interviews
    - At this time can the new company management team speak with the media?

Build your strategy

- Ongoing, continue to target long-leads, feature and response opportunities, thought leadership articles
- Preparation is key: solid Q & As, defined roles, mock interviews for handling questions, Sihabi and Mike to undergo media/messaging refresher

ROLL OUT

We prepared a detailed timetable so that everyone knew what was due to happen when, and could take responsibility for their part.

Timetable

Monday 5th pm	Run through of mock interviews
Tuesday 6th	
0800-900	FT breakfast briefing under embargo
0900	Staff announcement
0900-1000	Dow Jones/ WSJE/CNBC (under embargo)
0930	Release to ISE
1000-1100	*The Daily Telegraph*
1000	Far Seas and Far East Press Conference (handled out of Far Seas country with separate spokesperson)
1100-11.30	*The Times*
11.30-12.00	Reuters
12.00-12.30	IHT
1230-1300	Bloomberg
1300-1330	Associated Press
1330-1400	BBC Online
1400-1500	Trade Press Conference
Post 1500	CNN
Post 1500	BBC World
Post 1500	US Interviews
Wednesday 7th	
0620	Radio 4 *Today* Programme
1000	*The Economist*
Ongoing	Further UK, Global Interviews

REVIEW

A full and final review of events was discussed in a round-table meeting made up of representatives across the business. This included senior management, the communications team, HR and front line staff, (team leaders, managers and staff trade union representatives). They discussed these points:

- Measurement and evaluation / how did it go?
- What went well, what didn't?
- How can things be done better next time?
- How can you continue to improve the communication process and delivery?
- Respond appropriately to feedback

An Innovative Communication Strategy – what makes it different?

The Innovative Communicator will build a strategy that's a mixture of structure, disciplined framework and flexibility to hit the ground running and seize opportunities as they come – that makes it different. It is not about sticking to the script at all costs.

> ***There is no definitive script with humans and a strategy must be able to reflect human changes in the plans and adapt quickly.***

When circumstances change, strategy allows you to change with it, change quickly and change "live". Finally an Innovative Communicator will build into their strategy the ability to think on their feet, so that they can respond to and provide solutions for unforeseen or unscripted events as they unfold.

At Blue Sky we had two major events. The first event was to formally announce the strategic partnership to staff on 18 September led by the Far Seas leadership. The second event a week later was led by the Group Director where he took staff through the next steps, following the Far Seas event a week earlier.

For the first event three board directors from Far Seas were flying in from the Far East to meet and present to Blue Sky staff, many of whom would soon be transferring to them as new employees. I discovered about a week before the launch event that the decision had just been taken by Far Seas to endorse three of the *old* Blue Sky directors to join four Far Seas directors to make up the board structure of the new organisation (joint venture).

I immediately seized the opportunity and proposed at a key meeting that it would be in everyone's interest if the management on stage at the launch event on the day, included the three newly appointed Blue Sky directors as well. The Blue Sky directors were well liked and respected by staff and they were familiar faces. If they joined forces on stage with the new international management who were in effect strangers, their joint presence would give visible credibility and substance to the strategic partnership we were communicating and promoting, rather than hearing from just one half of the partnership who were strangers.

I persuaded the decision makers that a full quorum directors' team presentation to reflect a joint venture was the right option for this crucial launch event. So with just six days to go before the launch, we adjusted the entire communication strategy and plan so that the launch event was presented by the new joint team of directors from both Blue Sky and Far Seas, who were to make up the new organisation. They were received most favourably by staff.

Useful tips for building your communication strategy

The aim of communication is to raise the profile and understanding of your project, programme or business, while minimising any misunderstandings and inappropriate expectations.

Strong innovative effective communication enables a business to clearly articulate its change or transformation journey, from the way the business operates (now) to the way the business needs to operate (future), so that staff can see and feel the difference.

> *Good communication is a primary enabler of change and the success of a business will be heavily influenced by effective innovative communication.*

Therefore building a transformational framework to motivate staff is crucial.

The choice of the right communication vehicles is critical to both delivering and establishing commitment of staff or your target audience.

Your communication vehicles should:

- Provide a co-ordinated approach to ensure consistent messages about your project, programme or business are presented and feedback gathered effectively

- Assist in demonstrating senior management's commitment to the project, programme or business and determination to achieve delivery

- Provide a constructive environment for those affected to surface their issues and concerns and respond to them

- Work with and use existing in-house internal communication channels (if appropriate) and in addition create involvement specific bespoke communication channels that meet the needs of your people in the change or transformation journey

- Centre communications around business milestones, continually reinforcing key messages

- Measure success and feedback regularly

The building blocks of good communication – how to capture a strategy and plan

- An effective communication strategy and delivery plan should state its purpose in its introduction.

- The purpose should be immediately followed by a one page executive summary.

Build your strategy

- The strategy and plan should include six to eight key messages that the business wants to communicate to its people. Here is an example:

---

1. The Finance Transformation Programme (FTP) has three major aims:
   - to be clear about what Finance is doing at all times (clarity)
   - to simplify the way Finance is run (simplicity)
   - to add value to the work finance does for the business (value)

2. The programme is replacing the current variety of financial systems with one significantly enhanced system operating on a single database, supporting one set of common processes.

3. FTP is essential for us to meet regulatory requirements.

4. FTP is essential for us to meet International Accounting Standards being implemented throughout Europe.

5. FTP will enable significant improvements to the effectiveness and efficiency of managing business performance.

6. The business needs to ensure that our people have a motivational working environment with clear objectives and career progression is a key driver for the FTP programme.

7. Comprehensive training will be given as an integral part of the programme.

8. The programme will give full support to people who are relocating or losing their jobs.

- There should be a set of guiding principles that drives the business communication, and an approach that defines a robust communication process.

An example:

> - To ensure effective communication senior management will be involved and will act as role models.
>
> - Effective two-way communication vehicles will be provided.
>
> - The communication process will be managed to ensure it adds value to the programme and organisation.
>
> - Relationships with stakeholders will be built and maintained to support programme and business objectives.
>
> - Credit will be claimed for achievements. Problems will not be hidden or swept under the carpet.

The communication plan components

- The objectives to be met by communication should be clearly set out, together with communication roles and responsibilities.

- A plan should make it clear that successful implementation will require co-operation from senior management as well as pro-active participation from site project teams, for instance, (or whoever you need) to deliver high profile, fast track initiatives that make a difference and give authority, credibility and substance to your programme and business.

- Communication channels that will serve as delivery mechanisms for sending messages to, and receiving feedback from, stakeholders should be themed such as verbal, written, social media channels. The channel or vehicle, a description and frequency of delivery should be included.

Build your strategy

- There should be a strategy delivery action plan which details the *who, what, why, when* and *where* of all planned communication activity. If you need to communicate to different geographical sites, there should also be site-specific communication plans.

- I did a job where the business site strategy included consolidation of the business's property portfolio. In this case, I wrote the overarching communication strategy with the delivery and action plan, and then wrote eighteen site specific communication plans to compliment the parent strategy. This meant that the communication delivery across the country from the South East of England to Scotland was well planned, timely, co-ordinated and focussed to meet staff needs.

- It is vital to state clearly in the communication plan the challenges you and your business face. So for instance, in one FTSE 100 company I worked in, the challenge in communicating to all staff was that there was no one communication vehicle in or across the business, that could be used to reach all fifteen thousand employees at the same time. In addition, not everyone had intranet, email or audio access. At the same time the organisation's in-house internal communication team had stopped key communication channels as they undertook a review.

- State clearly in your plan what is out of scope. Companies, particularly big ones, are terrible at "scope creep". What scope creep does is to create ambiguity, confusion and chaos – what I call fudge and fog! People start becoming unclear about their remit of work, who is supposed to be doing what, and who is accountable for anything. There then tends to follow endless meetings to discuss the out of scope work that has somehow crept in, which means the work in scope loses focus, and the output more often than not is inevitably either ineffective, or non-existent because it didn't happen.

- You get my drift. It is vital to be clear about what is in scope and to be disciplined in staying within it. If other work needs to be included, it needs to be agreed and mandated in writing as a change request, so that the discipline drives and creates clarity.

- Finally, fundamental to overall success is the process of measurement, monitoring, adjusting and adapting communications to effectively meet changing needs. Measurement criteria should include objectives, how to define the objectives success and its measurement method.

An example:

Objective	Success defined as	Measurement method
Consistent message	Feedback from staff suggests they feel well informed. Conflicting messages are not circulated on the grapevine	Formal review of communication events by evaluating completed feedback questionnaires. Use existing vehicles
Senior management commitment	Communication event owned and fronted by senior managers	Communication and HR team to review and measure informally

Communication strategy goals

Your programme or business goals should include identifying all communication audiences, agreeing the key messages and delivery mediums, agreeing ownership for forming, approving, signing off and delivering the messages, assuring technical accuracy of the messages and agreeing the process for producing timely messages to all audiences.

Criteria

Your communication strategy and delivery plans should meet the following criteria:

- **Simple:** Clarity is all! Clear plain English and to-the-point messaging should be used. An overdose of corporate or project speak may lead to complications.

- **Harmonised:** Consistent in tone of voice and content, no mixed messages, jargon or acronyms.

- **Flexible:** To react to new developments, varied interpretations, commentary and industry announcements.

- **Consistent:** Style, tone and messages need to mirror one another internally, to the wider business audience and align with external communication.

- **Aligned:** The communication strategy and plan should align with other key business strategy including the business HR people engagement strategy (if there is one).

- **Flexibility:** As an Innovative Communicator you deliver communication that is agile and flexible, you quickly execute fresh ideas and solutions. You effectively join up complex and sensitive communication and you can spot, seize and act on new opportunities for the benefit of your business.

Building your strategy – summary

> An innovative communication strategy creates a transformational framework that keeps people at the heart of the business and keeps them motivated.
>
> The aim of your strategy is to raise the profile and understanding of your business, while minimising any misunderstandings or inappropriate expectations.
>
> The success of your business will be heavily influenced by effective innovative communication.
>
> Your communication output needs to be clear, harmonised, disciplined, flexible, consistent and aligned with the business strategy.
>
> Turn complex jargon into language everyone can understand and keep it simple.
>
> You are a collaborative player where required but equally prepared and able to create a communication strategy "from scratch" and make what needs to happen, happen.
>
> Measure, monitor, adjust and adapt your communication strategy to effectively meet changing needs.
>
> Seize opportunities that make a difference, think creatively and think outside the box if it is necessary, to be flexible in your strategy.

Questions to think about

- How might your business benefit from the approaches to building your strategy set out in this chapter?

- How could you put people "more at the heart" of your business?

- Who in your team would be the best "Innovative Communicator" to prioritise and implement "putting people at the heart of your strategy"?

Exercise

If you do one thing today, have a coffee with a front line member of staff who is on the receiving end of your company communication (someone you would normally not meet or associate with) and get some direct face-to-face feedback on their views.

5

Push your own boundaries

> *"Pushing your own boundaries to stretch beyond your comfort zone is vital for the development and growth of your communication skills. Do what you can, a step at a time."*
> **Miti Ampoma**

Chopping tomatoes, cleaning toilets and the £10.00 an hour job: how this pushed my boundaries and influenced my communication skills

In the early days of building my public relations and communication career, to keep body and soul together while applying for endless "real jobs", I worked in the kitchens of a well-known department store, cutting and chopping tomatoes for the customer restaurant by day and cleaning toilets by night. To meet the rigorous standards of the restaurant's department store, I was taught to cut and chop tomatoes in a specific way – into flawless star shapes – which I can assure you is quite an art form. I've cut hundreds and thousands of star-shaped tomatoes onto conveyor belts for inspection by beady-eyed duty managers. As a worker, I was expected to complete a significant quota of perfectly cut star-shaped tomatoes in every ten-hour shift. If a worker was no good at delivering the goods, they were sacked. It was that simple. As I couldn't afford the sack, I quickly learnt to become an expert at chopping and cutting brilliant star-shaped tomatoes. At the end of my tomato-cutting shift, I would join the hundreds and thousands of night workers at my second job of cleaning toilets. Again, I learnt to clean toilets brilliantly because I wanted to keep my job.

Gritting my teeth and learning to get on with cutting star-shaped tomatoes professionally (quite a skill albeit a mind-numbing one on an industrial kitchen conveyor belt), and cleaning toilets to the best of my ability, sticking with something, staying the course, doing it well and becoming an expert at it, for an honest income was invaluable training.

Throughout my experience doing these two jobs for a considerable length of time, my ability to relate to, interact with, and build a variety of relationships at various levels and communicate professionally with other tomato workers, toilet cleaners as well as the respective managers checking our work, was developed.

As in those early days, I still do jobs on low wages today to push my own boundaries. Every year or two, I make the time to spend up to twelve weeks doing a minimum wage job that pays a maximum of £10 an hour. I sign up to a temping agency where there are plenty of roles. My jobs have been wide and varied. I've worked as a secretary and junior assistant in offices through to working as a leaflet dropper on a bitter cold Friday winter evening in unfamiliar residential areas, dropping leaflets in letter boxes. In an eight-hour shift you do the job carrying heavily packed leaflets in a rucksack on your back, so you can leaflet drop quickly and efficiently. For £8 an hour these are long hours on low wages. So why do I do this and why is it relevant to communicating well in business?

Working on the front-line of a business for low wages is an experience that no classroom, book, education or clever communication strategy can give an Innovative Communicator.

The essence of an Innovative Communicator is to inhale, infuse and integrate direct human experience into the way they communicate with wisdom.

Working as a £10 an hour front-line administrator and being treated badly by a manager (who may not deem you important enough to treat you well) or getting to know permanent staff and listening to uncensored views of their senior executives and organisation, hearing their genuine cynicism, means I understand and have first-hand knowledge of the grassroots and front-line employees of a business. This means that when I write a communication strategy and plan for an organisations needs, my own direct experience informs my understanding of the frustrations of front-line staff on low wages. I am able to relate to them from a position of direct experience. This gives me the credibility and strong capability for building deep relationships with people in a similar position, because we genuinely have something in common and they are relieved they are working with someone they believe understands them and their perspective.

Why it's a good thing to push your own boundaries to become a better communicator

While I choose to push my own boundaries by working long hours for low wages at times, everyone can think of an activity they can do which will challenge them to do things differently and take them out of their comfort zone. Doing this develops and sharpens character as well as interactive skills with other people that you would not necessarily come into contact with, be around, speak to or necessarily be comfortable with. However, it is an invaluable rite of passage in developing great inter-personal interactive communication skills, influenced by direct human experience. In an environment that challenges and pushes your buttons, you are likely to develop invaluable interactive skills you can *drag and drop* and use time and time again to give your communication skills real advantage and power.

Helpful tips to enable you to think on your feet

- **Hold your nerve:** By taking up an activity (of your choice) that pushes your boundaries, you will find that you inevitably need to hold your nerve and not give up, as you will be in uncomfortable, unfamiliar territory and are likely to be tempted at some point to give up. Don't give up. You are not a quitter. Challenge yourself to complete the "push my boundary" activity you have set yourself. By finishing the task(s) you will hold your nerve and experience the benefits of learning to do so.

- **Drag and drop previous experiences:** Make a habit of digging deep into previous successful experiences that pushed your boundaries. Innovate by reliving and transferring these strategies into the challenging situation you face.

- **Knowledge and trust of self:** Listen to and trust your own gut instinct and intuition. It is often telling you something important about the way forward. If the feeling about something specific gnaws away inside you and won't go away, it's worth paying attention to it. Let it be your guide in making informed decisions and enabling you to find solutions.

- **Deliver results in a challenging environment:** Think of and hold on to your sense of achievement in making this happen. It'll be a positive, uplifting experience. It is worth soldiering on for. Go for it!

- **Curiosity to know more:** Develop the skill of wanting to know more. People love to talk or share something of themselves, their experiences or hobbies. Ask them questions. It really is a case of "seek and ye shall find" and it's amazing what you will find.

- **Provide relevant solutions that work:** Providing solutions that are relevant to people and the task, becomes an easier one to achieve when the vital subtleties, nuances and complexities that are our human makeup are better understood. The more you push your own boundaries and interact with a variety of people, going outside your comfort zone, the more experience you gain in understanding human complexities, and the more likely the solutions you provide for challenging issues will be relevant, workable and successful.

By pushing your own boundaries, the direct experiences you gain will make a difference to how you interact and engage with others and what you do to connect various disparate groups who would not necessarily come together or get on with each other.

These skills will evolve and develop, becoming a natural day-to-day communication activity, forming an innovative way of behaving rather than a prescriptive set of communication methodology.

You will emerge as a key player in your business because you are a lynchpin, a connecter, a facilitator and an energiser, simply by the way you behave, interact and communicate with others. This will distinguish you as an Innovative Communicator.

Working as a massage therapist: how this pushes my boundaries and influences my communication skills

In 2004 my boundary-pushing activity was deciding to train for a year as a clinical massage therapist and doing it. Doing lots of corporate communication work, I wanted to make sure I did not fall foul of becoming a corporate clone with developed corporate speak. I wanted to make sure I held on to the strengths of staying in touch with the human experience, so my corporate clients would benefit from this, because it influences and makes a difference to the quality and outcome of business communication programmes.

> **Staying in touch with the human experience is not a theoretical exercise. It is not achieved by writing up HR or management consultancy spreadsheets or power point diagrams on communication, nor by simply writing up value and mission statements. It is something that is done, felt, understood, and gained in the muscle.**

To be honest, when I signed up to train as a therapist I thought it would be easy. I mean how difficult could it be to learn how to stroke bodies appropriately? My first challenge was in discovering that I was expected to learn anatomy and physiology to GP level and pass exams in it to qualify. Given I had not done any biology since 'O' levels, my boundaries were truly pushed. I was required to massage and write up twenty detailed case studies of people I had worked with each month. The training also included practical massage work in hospitals and hospices. I worked in a hospice.

Massaging the terminally ill and offering palliative care is a privilege and a humbling experience. Witnessing the effect the power of touch can have on the terminally ill, be it massaging their feet, or back, is a powerful human experience. Building relationships with people coming to the end of their lives, listening to their life stories (some of whom had been senior executives in the business world), their joys and sorrows, and then going in the next week to find they had passed away puts life firmly in perspective. It gave me a strong sense of perspective and balance in terms of what is important and meaningful in the scheme of life.

So when I am in the business world with chaos reigning and people throwing their toys out of the pram in meetings about "issues", I strive to be centred and grounded and aim to bring solutions that add value for the good. In the scheme of things, life is too short and we should put energy into solutions.

For me, massaging the terminally ill in 2004, was a deeply profound human experience which has highly influenced my approach and style to business communication work, because it changed me as a human being and changed the way I see others.

Courageous conversations

My massage career has also been key in teaching me how to have a professionally difficult or courageous conversation.

One situation that springs to mind was at a hospice I worked in. As a trainee our job was simply to massage the patients and listen to them. However, with one elderly lady, I felt increasingly uncomfortable when I noticed she had bruises on her body. I asked her if she was alright and if the bruises hurt, as I did not want to cause her any further discomfort. She insisted she was alright and not to worry about her. I did not press her further, but my deepest intuition was worried and I felt all was not as it should be and I believed I should do something about it, rather than turn a blind eye. I took a deep breath and went to see the manager of the department. As a trainee, with this rare opportunity to massage in this well-known hospice, I felt scared about taking action. However, I knew the alternative would be far worse in that I would find it difficult if anything untoward happened to the elderly patient and I had not brought it to anyone's attention. Knocking in trepidation on the manager's door this is how the following "difficult dialogue" took place:

Manager: Come in!

Miti: Hello, My name's Miti. I'm one of the trainee therapists on the ward. I wondered if there was any possibility of a quick chat about something that's really bothering me.

Manager: Hello Miti, yes do come in. My name is Mary, how can I help?

Miti: *[Heart pounding, sits opposite manager]* I hope you'll forgive me if I'm speaking out of turn. I know as a trainee I'm just here to massage the patients. Nevertheless, I have noticed something that I'd never forgive myself for if matters took a turn for the worst and I hadn't said anything.

Manager: Go on.

Miti: In the last week since I've been massaging Mrs Smith, I've noticed that she's developed some bruises. First there were a couple on her arm and now there's definitely another one on her upper back near her shoulder. The only question I've asked is if it hurts as I want to avoid causing her any discomfort. All she says is that she is fine and doesn't want to be a bother. But the bruises look deep and fresh to me and I strongly feel something is wrong. I really wanted to quietly bring this to the attention of someone experienced. I don't want Mrs Smith to think I am telling tales about her, as we do get on very well, but I am very concerned with what I see. I hope it's alright to tell you.

Manager: Thank you Miti. I know the guidelines for trainees are strict but they are just guidelines and you have done the right thing in coming to me. I will take it from here.

Miti: My concern is I really would not want Mrs Smith to think I've snitched on her and for my training centre to think I'm behaving out of turn. I will of course be telling my own supervisor about this so they are kept in the loop.

Manager: Don't worry, Mrs Smith won't think you've been unfair to her. I will handle this myself. Thank you for letting me know. I'll have a word with your centre supervisor too. I'll let you know the outcome.

Miti: I left the office with my heart still pounding, scared but relieved, knowing in my deepest instinct that I had taken the right option, regardless of the outcome.

The outcome: *After taking over the matter herself, Mary the manager discovered that Mrs Smith lived on her own and that the emergency chord that connected her home to the outside world had broken. For a time her bedroom and corridor lights had blown too. Not having the emergency chord to seek help, she was going to the toilet in the night in the dark and kept bumping into furniture which was causing the bruising. She hadn't wanted to make a fuss, but she was distraught, burst into tears and told Mary how she relieved she was that Mary had asked her. The hospice arranged for her light bulbs and her emergency chord to be fixed right away. When Mary told me the outcome, I have to admit I had a weep myself, I was so relieved all round!*

When I fully utilise the experience of having a courageous conversation like this, when I drag and drop the building blocks, method and style, into the busy complex business world which is also made up of human beings, it brings a depth and additional dimension to my business communication programmes.

The added bonus is that I happily have a whole other career as a clinical massage therapist. I have worked at corporate events and functions, had my own private practice where I specialised in stress relief massage, worked in spa's and have done pro-bono work in a prison, the London marathon and for the Tsunami disaster appeal. Building relationships and communicating professionally with a wide variety of people beyond my immediate big business environment, continues to benefit my communication skills in business.

The point of this story is that it really stretched my boundaries. I was working in an environment in which I was the new kid on the block, not the expert. I was learning and I had to use communication, language, intuition and instinct in this unfamiliar environment to achieve the right outcome.

Tips to guide you when handling difficult requests

- Be gracious, courteous and respectful (this is not the same as being self-effacing or obsequious).

- Clearly explain the situation showing your concern and giving any facts you have gathered.

- Show respect for confidentiality.

- Act altruistically with a generosity of spirit.

- Be transparent and say it as it is from the heart.

- Speak to the best in the other person. After all, who doesn't want happy colleagues, customers and more profits?

Commit to continuous professional and personal development

By committing to continuous professional and personal development you will continue to learn and grow and this will shape your growth, maturity and ability to communicate effectively with others. Give both professional and personal development equal priority. One must not be at the expense of the other. It is important to grow personally in order to achieve professionally.

Block out the time to do the work required, no excuses. We all have 168 hours in the week to play with. Stay with the process. The rewards are worth it. There is a saying: Some drink at the fountain of knowledge, others just gargle. As an Innovative Communicator you definitely want to be drinking!

Aim for development and training courses which require you to do something and take action with goals, outcomes, purpose and achievements, as opposed to listening attentively to talks and lectures only. Unless you take part in activity, the temptation is to come home and put the manual of notes away to gather dust.

Pushing your own boundaries – summary

> Do at least one chunky activity a year that takes you out of your comfort zone, makes you feel uncomfortable and challenged because it is unfamiliar territory.
>
> Commit to meeting and working with another person (or group of people) you normally would not work with e.g. as a volunteer.
>
> Make the effort to network, socialise and meet people beyond your immediate professional circles.
>
> Mentally drag and drop your learning and growth acquired from pushing your boundaries into relevant and appropriate work situations. Know and appreciate the value of what you learn.
>
> Commit to ongoing personal and professional development and give them equal priority.
>
> Take a deep breath and be bold to be the Innovative Communicator you are meant to be.

Questions to think about

- What experiences have taken you out of your comfort zone and pushed your boundaries?

- Are you able to use any of the learning from this chapter or your own previous experiences, to help in delivering future outcomes in your business?

- Should you need to push your boundaries, what conversation(s) in the workplace might you initiate, to connect you with others you would not normally engage with? It may be with:

    - A single individual in your work place
    - People who work above your level
    - People who work below your level
    - Your employees in general

- What activity in your personal life over the next twelve months can you take part in to really challenge you?

Exercise

If you do one thing today, find a colleague in your business who has the opposite listening/talking skills to yours. If you are a natural listener challenge yourself to talk about a piece of work which concerns you, uninterrupted for fifteen to twenty minutes. Conversely, if you tend to be a natural talker, challenge yourself to listen to your colleague's work problem without interrupting them for fifteen to twenty minutes. Make sure you each have the opportunity to listen or talk, according to what you feel most uncomfortable doing. At the end of the exercise, review and discuss the reactions, thoughts and feelings you gained from the exercise with your colleague.

6

Step forward with courage

> *"If you tingle with challenge in a situation, find a way to stay calm and take appropriate action, you are courageous."* **Miti Ampoma**

Control, calm and clarity in the eye of the storm

I was called in by a large public relations agency to help them with their client, who was facing near mutiny from staff as a result of mismanaging the move of their headquarters. The organisation, which had been based in London for twenty years, had decided to move out of London to Southern England. The only problem was they had not quite got round to telling the staff, and with six weeks to go before the move, employees found out through the media. They were up in arms. The company, a global giant, had a parent company whose culture was used to issuing edicts that staff were expected to obey without question. So it proved a shock when they realised, that employees in their London office did not quite share their views of willy nilly obedience, and were in no mood to be readily compliant in uprooting their lives at six weeks' notice.

> **Mutiny was a big problem for the company because staff – and highly skilled ones at that – were refusing to relocate, something their leaders had astonishingly not factored into the equation of possible outcomes.**

The bottom line was no staff, no work output, no work output, no production, no production, no profits, no profits, no business.

Having allowed news of the move to reach staff via the media, the company had no communication plans in place to let staff know the details of the move either. Who was supposed to be moving when? Where exactly was the new headquarters? What did the new building look like? What preparations were required to vacate their iconic London headquarters where they had been for the past twenty years? No one knew and there was nothing in place to tell them. Chaos reigned, with rumours and corridor conversations rife. Staff were openly applying for jobs and off to job interviews. The company found itself in the eye of the storm, principally because it was so bad at communicating with its people.

With six weeks to go before a major move and with no communication plan in place, it was a case of getting to grips with the crises PDQ (pretty damn quick!). It was a potentially overwhelming situation and frankly my initial reaction was one of not a little depression, shock and incredulity at the mismanagement and resulting confusion and deep resentment of staff. Privately, I was not sure I could turn the situation around. The timelines were so tight. Having stepped into the fray and agreed to help though, I was determined to turn this "juggernaut" around, if I possibly could.

The first thing I did was to calm my mind. I did this by gradually but quickly mentally detaching myself from and letting go of my own personal reactions and emotions of shock, incredulity and not a little depression.

When all is reigning confusion around you, the best thing to do is still the mind and make this your top priority. It will prevent you becoming part of or falling into the maelstrom with everyone else. Take deep breaths and mentally visualise images of happier situations which bring calmer, soothing emotions back to your being. For me it is simply visualising some of the best beaches (the sea, the blue sky, the sun, the white sand) I have been to on holiday, along with some of the best sunsets I've seen around the world. Through practice, I have got these images fully in my mind, to draw on when all is falling around my ears. The more practice you give to this mental visualisation, the more it becomes the norm in your mind. Everyone can do this and have a great store of strong calming images in their mind to draw on whenever required. I did this exercise in the workplace most days and practiced it consciously for about ten minutes each evening when I got home during those early chaotic days.

This very simple technique has time and time again placed my frame of mind and physiology in the right place to equip me to cope well with overwhelming pressure. The huge and critical benefit of the exercise is it makes you calm so you can think objectively and communicate clearly, calmly and professionally – effectively communicating your way through chaos – and that's the result that's needed.

So back to my global client and the crises we faced!

On my first day I had a meeting with the PR agency partner and the Managing Director (MD) of the company. Civil and charming as the meeting was, by asking him politely clear, concise and simple questions, I quickly worked out that sadly, the MD himself was largely the problem. He was the blocker for getting anything done. He ran the business with a level of near paranoid secrecy which took lack of information and communication in a business to new heights. My brief which was his brief, was to fix the problem of his people being up in arms, but he did not want me to speak to any of his senior team because "It wasn't the way we do things round here". In fact it soon transpired that nobody was allowed to speak to any of his senior team. There was such a big hierarchical gap literally and psychologically within the business it gnawed like an open wound. "It's not the way we do things round here" was his standard response for most questions and requests. In short, he sounded like a stuck record.

At the end of the meeting the MD announced he was going on holiday for two weeks, and as my agency client partner was also leaving for holiday that afternoon, I was put in charge for the next two weeks. I said a silent prayer of thanks, despite no handover. Once I was in charge, I hit the ground sprinting with a communication strategy and action plan to resolve the mess.

Having been barred by the MD himself from contacting his senior management, I respected and honoured his instruction. Instead I contacted the next layer of management that I had not been barred from, that is, the direct reports of the senior management and talked to them in detail. It was no surprise to me that they were gasping to talk!

The Innovative Communicator

Their views and feedback was most instructive and confirmed my initial view of the source of the problem. I knew then that if the problems we faced were to be fixed, I had to seize the opportunity of the next ten days, while I was in charge, to make things happen.

Over the next ten days, armed with the views, and feedback of the managers, I quickly built strong rapport and good relations with them and got them on side. With their support, I produced a detailed communication countdown planner for the various phases of the move from London to the new headquarters in Southern England. There was to be a move every week for a month. The research I had done, with all the relevant stakeholders meant I had an unrivalled knowledge of the move end-to-end. So the countdown planner included details like the role IT were playing in helping people with their computers and laptops, right through to the allocation of new staff telephone numbers.

I set up briefing sessions and move workshops and having built strong relationships with staff, persuaded a group of people to fulfil the role of Move Liaison Officers, making the role come alive. We organised and put together move packs with content to explain details such as check-lists, useful tips for their move and plans for their travel arrangements. For the travel arrangements we produced a route map, a travel itinerary and a Frequently Asked Questions pack on the company's intranet site and Q & A database. This information clearly told staff what they needed to do in London before they moved, for example archiving and shredding, arrangements for packing crates to arrive on site and timelines for packing. We gave staff a dress down day to do their packing. At the new offices they had a Welcome Pack on each desk on arrival. We produced a pocket guide they could easily carry and advised them to do a recce test-run to the new headquarters in Southern England, so they were confident of how to get there before their move date.

The biggest role innovative and effective communication played however, was in persuading the staff that moving to South England was seriously worth considering as an option. Effective communication was central to turning round this seemingly insurmountable juggernaut of mutiny. So how did this happen?

I had gone around the business with speed and within days built strong relationships with many of the employees by listening to them, their grievances and resentments, hopes and fears and by finding something I had in common with them to connect us and enable meaningful dialogue. This calmed many of them down visibly as they felt there was someone listening to them at last. They simply needed to be heard, not ignored and made to feel irrelevant. Having built deep personal relationships across the business very quickly, I created and delivered a company newsletter updating staff fully about what was happening.

Through the front line staff who I had now got on side, I found a few people who were willing to relocate if the right conversations were had, and through them I hit bingo by finding a couple who had initially been very reluctant to move from London, had almost quit the company and then changed their minds after driving around the surrounding areas of their would-be new location. At first they had described the company's new location as a "sort of one horse town" without having been there, but once they visited they realised "how wrong we've been. We absolutely love it," they said to me as we chatted over a cup of tea. They had made the decision to make the move and swapped their two bedroom flat in London for a three-bedroom cottage with a cellar, garden and two bathrooms in Southern England. They joked that they had more friends and family coming to stay with them in their new home than they did in London because they now had space and were thinking of charging bed and breakfast rates as there was always someone staying with them. They enthused "We're just fifteen minutes drive from work and the drive to work is like something out of the Darling Buds of May – all rolling fields and woodlands. It's great. And if we want to go up to London it's only twenty minutes to Kings Cross". Of the company they added "We think it's a very exciting time for the company and we want to be part of it. The company is spending almost £100 million and that's very exciting. It would be silly to leave a company that's investing that much and growing so much. There are going to be lots of opportunities".

My heart was pounding with excitement as I listened to this couple. I knew they were highly respected by their colleagues in the business and having spoken with them at length, I knew instinctively that they were my golden passport to resolving our crises and turning the juggernaut. I persuaded them to tell their story and they happily obliged. I immediately put together a newsletter special and wrote a double spread feature about them. I simply let them be the ambassadors for the company and communicate another perspective of the situation at hand. Their published interview was indeed the turning point. Once the other employees read about these friends and colleagues who had made the decision to move and relocate, they too were prepared to enter into conversation about the possibility of relocating too. The end result was that the majority of staff agreed to relocate. We had cracked it. By the time the MD returned from his two-week holiday, his problem was fixed. My client partner from the agency was ecstatic and it was a win-win all round. Result!

The point of this story is that matters were satisfactorily resolved primarily through dealing with the maelstrom by communicating innovatively. Communicating effectively through the chaos was central to achieving a successful outcome.

A tricky dialogue with the Managing Director, Kevin

Often we are faced with tricky conversations, in which we may have to gain the trust of another person, and this was a particular case in point in the relocation case study above. This conversation needed dollops of courage, because my task was to prepare the ground to gain trust when faced with considerable obstacles, namely:

- Kevin was the Managing Director.

- He was set in his ways and assumed his staff understood what he wanted.

- He was off on holiday at a critical time.

- My task was to find an innovative solution in his absence, to solve his challenging dilemma.

Miti and agency client partner Bob arrive at Kevin's office:

MD: Good afternoon Bob, you must be Miti, thank you for coming.

Bob: Hello Kevin, good to see you, yes this is Miti.

Kevin: Do sit down. *[Guides us with his eyes to our seats]*

Step forward with courage

Kevin: So, we have a problem, the troops don't seem to want to move and we don't have a lot of time left to get them to do this.

Miti: Hello Kevin, good to meet you. Sorry to hear about the troops! Could I ask, would you mind explaining even briefly what's happened, what the current mood's like in your opinion and what preparation and communication is in place so far?

Kevin: Well things could be a lot better. As senior executives we made a decision to move our headquarters to Southern England, as it's more cost effective and we get more space for our money in the new office park. We've not got any communication in place, the timetable there has sort of slipped which is why we called in Bob's agency. We recognise we should be getting on with things.

Miti: *[In a supportive gracious tone]* I understand this must be a difficult time for you. Could I ask, when you say you have no communication in place, do you mean there isn't a person in charge, or do you mean there isn't a plan?

Kevin: Well HR have done some bits, but nothing is co-ordinated. We tend to buy in communication skills as we need them.

Miti: OK, but given our critical timescales, we need to put an action plan together. Would it be helpful if I spoke to your senior team to quickly get their views and perspectives on the situation, and a clearer sense of the mood in their departments?

Kevin: *[Sharp intake of breath]* Oh no, I'm not sure speaking with any of my senior direct reports is a good idea. It doesn't really work that way. It's not the way we do things round here.

Bob: *[Looking weary]* Well Kevin, we don't have much time left and it would be useful to be able to speak your team as they are leaders of your various departments.

Kevin: No, I'm not comfortable with that. It's not the way we do things round here. I'm also going on holiday this evening and I'm away for two weeks, so speaking with my senior team wouldn't work.

Miti: *[Realising this is going to produce a sleepless night!]* Oh, I hope you're going somewhere nice! So what's your biggest concern right now?

Kevin: Well I need to get the workforce back on side and for most of them to relocate. Some of them are highly skilled and it'll be difficult to replace them. I also need a really good communications programme because we have nothing at the moment and this is a problem for us now.

Bob: I'm off on holiday tomorrow too!

Kevin: Sorry to do this to you Miti, but you'll have to take charge. Apologies for the short notice.

Miti: *[With heart in mouth but keeping a cheery smile]* Don't worry while you're away we'll work as team. We'll sit down and develop a solid strategy and action plan. To reassure you, is there someone in particular you'd like me to keep informed of progress?

Kevin: If you keep Bob's PR colleague at the agency informed that'll be great. Good I'm glad that's all sorted then. Miti, good to have you on board. Hope it goes well in the next couple of weeks. I look forward to progress on my return.

Miti: Great, have a lovely holiday. Leave things with me and I'm confident we'll come up with an action plan that'll work.

Helpful tips to get someone on side

- Allow the other person to voice their story, opinions and actions.

- Ask probing questions respectfully.

- Precede further probing questions with empathy and acknowledgement of what you've just been told.

- Express a way forward using inclusive language – *we* and *our*.

Step forward with courage

- Gently take control by offering your opinion as a helpful suggestion.

- Build trust by reassuring what *we* will do.

- Ensure you agree on how you remain accountable.

Postscript – post holiday conversation

Kevin: *[In his office with Miti]*: Congratulations, I can see lots of progress has been made and we are set to go.

Miti: Yes, it's been a great team effort by everyone. Here is a pack of all the literature we've produced to help people with the move.

Kevin: *[In softer than usual tone]* I've had great feedback about the role you've played in making this move happen Miti. In fairness, I had no idea that communication could play such an instrumental part in my business. I wanted to apologise for being rather unhelpful before I left. I want to thank you again.

Miti: Don't worry Kevin, it's not a problem. I'm just glad it's all worked out for the best. I hope you'll be very happy in your new location. Take care.

Strategies for courage

Having strategies for courage is something we can learn to do. It does not happen by genetics or luck. There are all kinds of stressful situations that require communicating with courage and calmness and you can change your state to achieve this.

- **Remember being brave:** Think of a time and situation when you were really up against it but were brave in your actions and came through the other end, to an outcome that was the right one all round. It doesn't matter the size of the situation, it can be big or small. How did the situation unfold? What did you actually do? What step(s) did you take that you later realised were brave? How did you feel? Relive each block of your successful story in bite-size chunks in your mind and being, and mentally drag and drop these skills you used so well into your current situation.

- **See yourself succeeding:** Reflect on times you found courage inside yourself that you did not know you had and drag and drop what you did, the way you felt, and the successful outcome of your courageous behaviour into your current moment. See yourself as courageous. Make it an identity statement. Start making important decisions that propel change, invite self observation and start getting rid of stories and thoughts that reinforce your view of what's not possible. Think about what is possible in difficult times. Trust that you can handle whatever comes next.

- **Calm your mind and being:** Make the calming and stilling of your mind your top priority amidst the chaos and confusion. Take deep breaths and mentally visualise images of happier situations which bring calmer, soothing emotions back to your being. Gradually but quickly mentally detach yourself from and let go of your personal reaction and emotions to the situation. Stay in the moment with the feelings and mental images that keep you calm and centred.

- **Break tasks into bite-sized chunks:** With a calmer mind, focus on chipping away at one task at a time rather than letting the big picture of what needs to be achieved overwhelm you. Talk to a friend who is a calm and balanced listener. It'll make you feel better. Take a break from the technology and leave your computer screen. Take a five minute walk or get a cup of tea. It all helps.

- **Take action:** Courage is all about taking action and doing something to make things happen. So take a deep breath and be a doer. The worst that can happen, is that you learn through experience and that in itself is a benefit. Taking action will move and change your circumstances, which is what courage is about.

- **Be bold and determined**: Hold on. Imagine a rope you are gripping and holding with both hands for dear life because below is a sheer drop. You will hang on to that rope to save yourself if your life depended on it. Being bold and determined holds that same energy and space. Bear with fortitude and soldier on.

- **Persevere:** You are not a quitter. You apply steady persistence in the course of action in spite of difficulties, obstacles or discouragement. Whatever the hurdles, you keep going. It will be fine in the end.

Seizing an opportunity with courage

A vital part of innovative communication is to be bold and seize opportunities when they come your way. An opportunity is won or lost in a moment. This can be the difference between the golden solution and nothing changing. So if you're feeling afraid but are tingling with challenge, step forward with courage.

When I first started learning and getting to grips with smart phones, social media and new technology it was frankly a struggle. I got some professional help to learn the basics, but of course with these things it is only by practicing and doing it yourself that the real learning and understanding takes off.

> *In the early days of learning, my social media teacher told me that I should take pictures with my smart phone camera at important business functions to post on my website. The thought left me terrified.*

I'm a wordsmith. Give me a book of 1000 pages and I can write an accurate synopsis of it with joy, no problem. Give me technology and I am likely to go into meltdown (desperately persevering with the "I can", rather than the "I cannot" strategies ☺).

So it was in the early days, that I found myself at a particularly important business function ironically on Social Media, with some key leading speakers. As the speakers took it in turns to speak and offer an abundance of knowledge, it struck me that it would be a great opportunity to have my picture taken with them on my smart phone, and get their permission to use it on my social media platforms.

> *A large part of me didn't want to do it, but a voice in my head and my intuition was saying, if you don't seize this opportunity you are not doing yourself justice.*

So as the guest speakers concluded their session and the evening came to a final close, I whispered to the complete stranger next to me and asked her if she would take a picture of me and the four guest speakers if I asked them. I then showed her quickly how to use my smart phone camera! My heart pounding I leapt to the front of the stage and caught the guest speakers just as they were leaving.

"Gentlemen," I smiled sweetly at them "I'm a novice at Social Media, trying to get to grips with it all, and my homework is to take a picture of me at this event on my smart phone and post it on my website. Is there any chance I could have my picture taken with you? I, and not least my social media teacher, would be joyous," I added. They were delighted and chorused "Of course!". And so I had several pictures of myself and four leading national social media experts at a key business function on my smart phone, despite my fear, and the potential difficulties of having my picture taken with these top experts in their field. I felt so chuffed as I stared at the pictures on my smart phone on the tube home. Result! As I told this story to a friend, she said to me, "Gosh Miti you are brave".

> *I had not thought of it as a brave thing to do at all, so having had it pointed out to me, I have subsequently analysed and relived the steps I took – what I did, how I did what I did, what I saw, how I felt and my sense of achievement at the outcome*

I have *bottled* this experience to draw on when I am in a future situation which requires me to be equally brave in spirit, in seizing an opportunity, in taking action and in communicating effectively through it all, to achieve a desired outcome.

Stepping forward with courage – summary

> Strategies for courage is something we can all learn to do and master.
>
> Make the calming and stilling of your mind your top priority amidst chaos and confusion.
>
> Reflect on a time when you were brave, even though at the time you might not have been aware of being brave. Use the experience to benefit an action in a difficult situation.
>
> Draw on times when you found courage inside yourself that you did not know you had. See yourself as courageous. Make it an identity statement and think about what is possible in difficult times.
>
> Take a deep breath and take action. Courage is all about taking action and propelling change.
>
> Keep going and do not give up. Perseverance is about steady persistence in the course of action in spite of difficulties. It will pay off.

Questions to think about

- Think of a time when you stepped forward with courage. In what way did you benefit from the experience?

- Is there a work situation that might benefit from the process by which you have shown courage in the past?

- Are you able to use any of the learning in this chapter to deliver future outcomes in your business? It may be with:

    - A single individual in your work place

    - People who work above your level

    - People who work below your level

    - Your employees in general

Exercise

If you do one thing today, contact someone in another part of your business, about a challenging issue you face. But first, pause the press button on any resistance you feel, take a deep breath, take courage in both hands, step into their shoes for a moment and dig deep for some human compassion whatever the situation. Know that the bottom line is, everyone wants to be heard and valued and every one wants things to work out well.

7

Get tough with heart

> *"Practise getting tough with heart through communicating innovatively and effectively instead of merely paying lip service to it, and all will be well whatever the business weather."* **Miti Ampoma**

We don't do "fluffy" stuff

There is often a sense by staff and the public (confirmed by many surveys) that the words "heart" and "feeling" are not natural affiliates to large-scale business communication. Indeed, I experience this to be true time and time again.

When I introduce the concept of "tough with heart" to senior management when looking at their communication woes, the atmosphere in the room tends to gravitate to one of "rabbit in headlights". Their eyes often widen in shock, they look uncomfortable, and they clearly wonder why they have agreed to hire me and, I suspect, worry I may be a little bonkers! So persuading senior management that "heart" is important when communicating tough messages, that un-British as it may be to "do emotion", let alone do so "at work", that it really is in their interest to try it, is a tough ask.

> *Many large businesses dub communication a "soft skill", but there is nothing soft about the ability and skills to communicate and articulate in such a way that people are bought into your goals for success. It is those very skills that drive performance in a business.*

The initial reaction to a "tough with heart" approach often results with one, some or all of the following:

- Hostility – What's the point? Why would we want to do that?

- That approach is soft and emotional – It won't work.

- Too busy, no time, diary chock-a-block.

- Haven't got time/don't want to meet with other executives or management on this particular topic – for example planning the way in which the news will be delivered as a team.

Simply put, when the messages that need delivering are unpalatable, avoidance tactics are rife.

> ***Delivering tough messages is an uncomfortable place to be. It's therefore too easy to deliver it in the easiest, quickest possible way rather than the best way.***

The quick but insensitive one-size-fits-all email or voicemail can prove the short-sighted saviour. The worst scenario of course is not delivering the news at all, with staff finding out through the media. In cases like this, staff perceive it as "paying lip service" or engaging in a "tick-box exercise", which simply alienates people and results in the sort of newspaper headlines businesses want to avoid.

Get tough with heart

A case in point

I read the following newspaper article on 8 March 2012 in *The London Evening Standard*. I would like to thank *The London Evening Standard* for their kind permission to reproduce it here.

Redundancy plans the KPMG way – by voicemail
By Lucy Tobin

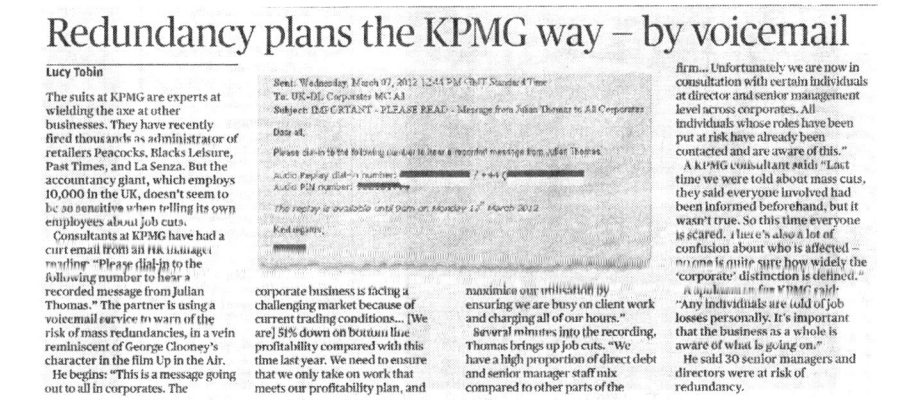

This article is © The London Evening Standard / writer Lucy Tobin, 8 March 2012

The article reads as follows:

> "The suits at KPMG are experts at wielding the axe at other businesses. They have recently fired thousands as administrator of retailers Peacocks, Blacks Leisure, Past Times, and La Senza. But the accountancy giant, which employs 10,000 in the UK, doesn't seem to be so sensitive when telling its own employees about job cuts.
>
> Consultants at KPMG have had a curt email from an HR manager reading: "Please dial-in to the following number to hear a recorded message from Julian Thomas". The partner is using a voicemail service to warn of the risk of mass redundancies, in a vein reminiscent of George Clooney's character in the film Up in the Air.
>
> He begins: "This is a message going out to all in corporates. The corporate business is facing a challenging market because of current trading conditions . . . (We are) 51% down on bottom line profitability compared with this time last year. We need to ensure that we only take on work that meets our profitability plan, and maximise our

> utilisation by ensuring we are busy on client work and charging all of our hours"
>
> Several minutes into the recording, Thomas brings up job cuts. "We have a high proportion of direct debt and senior manager staff mix compared to other parts of the firm . . . Unfortunately we are now in consultation with certain individuals at director and senior management level across corporates. All individuals whose roles have been put at risk have already been contacted and are aware of this".
>
> A KPMG consultant said; "Last time we were told about mass cuts, they said everyone involved had been informed beforehand, but it wasn't true. So this time everyone is scared. There's also a lot of confusion about who is affected – no one is quite sure how widely the 'corporate' distinction is defined".
>
> A spokesman for KPMG said: "Any individuals are told of job losses personally. It's important that the business as a whole is aware of what is going on".
>
> He said 30 senior managers and directors were at risk of redundancy.

It is tough to lose your job. Surely anyone who finds themselves in this situation deserves compassion and consideration in the way in which they receive that news. None of us is exempt from this potentially unfortunate fate. Who doesn't want to be treated with respect and sensitivity when the going gets tough? We all do of course. It is a basic human need.

Key factors in getting tough with heart

Getting tough with heart is not about the kind of routine hiring and firing that HR does, such as calling someone into the office for "the chat". It's about the bigger picture within the organisation – when grim news has to be announced to a potentially very large workforce, by its directors.

There has to be a clear, bold communication strategy which puts *people* at the centre, and this involves:

- Drawing up a face-to-face communication programme that respects people and gets them on board. This means eyeball contact between human beings!

Get tough with heart

- Facing the music, taking responsibility with wisdom, courage and understanding.

- Delivering grim news honestly, clearly with sensitivity and compassion, however emotionally difficult this may be.

- Committing to play your part in supporting your impacted people, being efficient, well prepared and there for them.

- Doing what you say you will do.

It is perfectly possible to gain the respect and co-operation of staff – against all odds – about tough decisions that impact them adversely. In my experience *it works* when those tough decisions are communicated well, communicated authentically and communicated with heart.

The benefits of "getting it right" are:

- The blow is softened and made more palatable.

- Loyal staff, who benefit emotionally through having been respected.

- Staff who come on side even in a crisis, roll up their sleeves and make things happen regardless of the knowledge they hold about their own grim future.

Communicate innovatively and effectively and it will be well, whatever the business weather!

I use the word 'innovative' here because in many large organisations, the idea of communicating with heart is *new!* In fact, what we are really talking about is good old-fashioned common sense. I know from personal experience, it is an 'innovative' communication programme that holds the business together and allows it to flourish in a time of crisis. It is the critical function that enables survival.

I created and delivered a major communication programme for a large blue chip client who had taken over a company whose employees were in shock at the reality of being acquired. The company being taken over had existed for almost fifty-five years and had a distinctive culture and close-knit family community ethos they were proud of. Being taken over by a FTSE 100 company was their worst nightmare come true.

Within a year of being taken over their new parent company was to let them know that they were making a majority of them redundant and transferring the remaining workforce to a new joint venture partner. It was the end of their world as they knew it.

I was brought in to help create a bespoke communication programme for a scheduled announcement of redundancies and the journey their people were about to embark on.

Having arrived and with just six weeks to go before the major redundancy announcement, I discovered not unusually, that there were almost no plans or practical arrangements in place for this impending redundancy announcement, with the exception of the date in the diary. Managers had been informed that this was a date they should mark in their diaries for their teams, so expectations were already set. However in practice there was nothing in place to support this date – a classic case of setting up for failure.

Where was the redundancy announcement "event" to be held? Had anyone got a venue? Who was in charge of the big picture and the small detail arrangements? Who would be speaking? Were senior executives involved? What role were managers playing? What was the plan for staff straight after they were informed of their redundancies? These questions urgently needed addressing.

My first priority was to project manage the practical preparations of the announcement after quickly building strong relationships in the business with those I needed on side. Within ten days, venue searches were organised and a suitable venue found and booked.

Senior executives were advised and coached in what they would need to say and how they were going to deliver the facts with compassion and sensitivity. We had sessions most weeks for about an hour and a half to two hours every week to support them.

Getting into their busy diaries was tough but achieved nevertheless. Having excellent relationships with PAs and executive assistants makes an awful lot possible. If a diary date was cancelled I was right on top of it and instantly rearranged, otherwise there was a danger of it not happening. Drift or delay is an absolute no no! I advised, influenced and persuaded the executive board to turn up in person and be on stage for the announcement to the impacted workforce and to take questions head on and answer them as fully as possible.

It was hard graft, but it paid off – they were fantastic, they got up on stage and delivered the news as one collective voice, with dignity compassion and sensitivity towards their people.

On the day of the announcement the impacted staff, who largely operated a business call centre, were taken off the phones to attend the announcement sessions. During the event, staff were able to ask whatever questions they liked to their leaders face to face. The Director of Human Resources (also a member of the executive board) was excellent at answering questions on the detail of redundancy packages.

At the end of the session, staff were not expected to go back on the phones and start working immediately with customers. This is critical and this is getting tough with heart. It makes a huge difference to be compassionate in this way when delivering this kind of tough news.

What is achieved by this is gaining the long term buy-in and good will of people who need to work hard for the business over a considerable period of time, despite the nemesis of their own redundancy.

Simply put, if you were told you were being made redundant, would you not need a little time off just to process it? Many large organisations give their staff this kind of shock news and then tell them to get back on the phones or get straight back to their work to continue "to do their best for the business". There is no time built in to digest the news or draw breath! Many staff finding themselves in this situation have described it as "jaw dropping insensitivity" leaving them and their colleagues unhappy, disgruntled, unvalued and unwilling to do their best for the business in the time they have left until their redundancy. Thoughtful considerations like giving time to process bad news are what people remember and talk about.

The announcement about the redundancies and the seismic changes ahead in which senior management were visible and accountable, set the tone for the rest of the communication programme in which some very tough messages and equally tough "to dos" were required to meet business goals and plans.

It was a tone of "we are all in this together and we are in this to make it work, regardless of how tough it might be". This tone resonated with staff and did so because they felt it, believed it and therefore emotionally benefitted from it.

The redundancy programme, the scaling down of the old company and the joint venture deal transferring remaining employees to a new company took about fifteen months. It was a long, tough, difficult, challenging, often sad journey for many workers who had been part of a loyal close knit family firm that was being broken up. But at the heart of the communication success was honesty, clarity, conviction and compassion in how we articulated and delivered the tough medicine from which there was no escape.

At each stage of the redundancy transformation journey, staff were kept informed regularly and consistently with a co-ordinated and integrated mix of direct messages. This was done through a variety of carefully chosen communication channels (for example through roadshows, news letters, workshops, conferences and one to one briefings) in order to deliver maximum impact for senior management. We nominated front-line team leaders and managers who were trusted by their colleagues. They were trained and equipped with innovative communication skills to support their colleagues facing difficult times. We set up specific local co-ordination teams and staff representative boards across the business and worked very closely with HR to craft all communication materials, so it was not just a spill and release of clinical data and process, but instead clear, accurate facts delivered with understanding and compassion.

None of the activities was lip service. It was not something we said we believed in and passively drew lovely posters to stick around the business for the affected to read! We actually took action. Day in and day out we grafted to give staff the best possible experience in extremely difficult times. The doing, gave the communication programme and therefore the leadership of the business credibility and authority when they spoke to their people about what the tough decisions meant, as well as the journey they faced together.

The proof of our "tough with heart" communication success was that the required performance was there in bucket loads. As staff experienced the emotional benefits of our actions during their tough times, they felt genuinely respected and valued, despite their trauma.

They stayed on side despite their own personal circumstances because they could see and feel that their executives and management were with them all the way amid the rubble of difficult decisions. They reciprocated in kind by working with pride and extremely hard to the very end. During the exit transition phase their unwavering commitment and professionalism was inspiring.

All key performance indicators and business targets were met. In short, despite their personal loss, the work of staff facing redundancy increased productivity and profits, up until the day they were forced to leave.

As staff lost their jobs, we had also put in place a contingency external communication strategy and action plan to deal with any potential fall out in relation to the media, should an unhappy employee decide to speak negatively to the press about events in the business. It was a tribute to staff and all the Innovative Communicators across the business that no member of staff went to the press. On the contrary, one of the key outputs and feedback from exiting staff, amidst tears and sadness was the consistent acknowledgement that they had been "proud to work as hard as they did because they were treated so well right through the trauma of losing their jobs".

One staff member added, "If I'm going to be made redundant, this is the way it should be done".

This is the result every business should strive to achieve. It's good for those leaving and therefore good for the external reputation of the business and it's great for the staff staying who see the way their colleagues are treated and encourages them to continue to make an effort for the good of the business, because they too will be treated well in tough times. It's a win-win all round.

Delivering the toughest news

What follows is a description of the grim news that had to be communicated to staff by their Senior Management (in the case study described).

A series of carefully arranged briefings, set up for retail operational colleagues impacted by a potential strategic partnership with a global information solutions company, is arranged over three days.

At each of these face-to-face briefings, speaking directly to the impacted workforce is Adam White, Change and Transformation Director, Harry Blue, Director of Human Resources and Communication and Kirsty Star, Head of Customer Contact Centre.

- Adam explains why the company changes are happening, how the staff may be potentially affected, what the company is doing to support them during this difficult period and the decision-making process that is underway.

- Harry outlines the legal requirements and HR implications regarding these changes. These will include the status of current terms and conditions, pensions, entitlements or benefits, and an outplacement programme which will assist staff who lose their jobs.

- Kirsty shares what the operational areas need to focus on at this challenging time, how management will support them and reward their loyalty.

Adam is on stage talking face-to-face with staff as their leader in a conversational empathetic style with minimum Power-Point slides. His tone is understanding and compassionate.

Adam: Good afternoon everyone. Thank you for attending and welcome. I'm Adam White and today, I'd like to take the opportunity to share with you, some of the most recent developments of our Transformation Programme. It's fair to say that we are about to embark on the most demanding times in our company's history. I know that many of you are feeling apprehensive about what this will mean for you and your colleagues and feeling this way is not unusual or wrong – it's human.

[Harry and Kirsty are also on stage listening]
Firstly, I'd like to welcome Harry Blue and Kirsty Star, whom you all know. They'll be helping me give you as much information as possible this afternoon.

[Being honest, clear and straightforward]
The Executive team and I are aware of the hard work and effort you have put into this company and we don't by any means expect thanks from you for the changes we'll be introducing through Transformation. There's no question that the change is tough though unfortunately necessary.

So in my section today, I want to talk about why Transformation is happening, what new technology will help us transform and how this will potentially impact your roles within our business.

Firstly, What is Transformation going to achieve?

We must build a winning business with leading partners to drive our market. Why? Because we must change to survive in a fast paced ever-changing marketplace.

The speed of technology is phenomenal and to bring home the impact it has on our business I'd like to use an analogy very close to home.

[Explaining in clear pictorial terms the background and the current situation]
Let me take you back to 1955 when our company was first established here in Riverside. Riverside Road was all factory buildings. Sainsburys in town had individual counters with manual workers and nothing was computerised. My first job included working in this very building.

Fifty-three years on, we have technological advances, sophisticated computers, smart phones and software enabling credit decision making. Around us are competitors selling digital TV and home computers and there is Internet shopping delivery to your door.

Although we have moved along since Riverside was established, we haven't moved at the pace we need to. Imagine, a bank today with no cash point machine for customers. It's unthinkable. Yet we've become the equivalent in our industry. We still have manual, multiple system platforms, we focus on price and we have poor measurement.

[Explaining logically what is needed]
We need to build a business equipped to survive the future. This has to be continually evolving and changing to keep pace with the times. We need to move to an automated, single system platform business with a focus on value, partnerships and robust measurement. Competition is fierce and is coming from new angles and channels like the Internet. Unless we change to suit the market, there is the real danger we won't have a business.

On our side however, there are other companies who specialise in top-notch technology solely on the areas of the business that we need to manage more effectively and efficiently.

This technology includes electronic point of sale (ePOS), Interactive Voice Recognition and Document scanning.

[He explains each of these technologies in more detail].
The benefits for our business is that there is less manual work and time required. The outcome in human terms is that fewer roles will be required to do or run the same or similar processes.

[He moves on to introduce the plan to merge]
We currently do many things quite well (we're a "Jack of all trades, master of none") but in order to build a winning business we must completely focus on what were are best at and master of. What we are best at is developing strong

Get tough with heart

partnerships with retailers through a clear understanding of the retail market. To help us focus on being this, we are working with an external company – Match – whose sole purpose is to provide operational services to businesses like ours. This potentially affects all the operational areas as all processes may be significantly changed and re-engineered to fit our future organisation. We are expecting to sign a contract in the middle of May.

What this does mean is that potentially, you will transfer to a new company which will be formed called Riverside Match Services which will involve both Riverside and Match.

On transfer your terms and conditions will be protected. Harry will go into the HR details in a few minutes.

[He predicts their question and answers honestly]
My guess is that now your question is, if terms and conditions won't change, why have we all been told that a significant number of roles will eventually disappear? This unfortunately, isn't a myth . . .

As the introduction of electronic point of sale, interactive voice recognition and document scanning come into full effect, and Match gain experience in handling the work, our Riverside operational roles will need to become fewer and work will transfer to Match – that's to say – roles undertaken by Match will not be the same as you are doing today.

We anticipate that around 80% of the operational areas will be affected by redundancies.

[Predicts their queries and gives appropriate reassurance]
However you can be assured that no redundancies will take effect until at least 1st September and the majority of redundancies will take place in fifteen months time.

[Paints a clear picture of what things will look like in the future, giving staff a chance to visualise and see how they might be affected]

By 2009 and beyond, Riverside will look very different. We will be focused on value-added activity that delivers business benefit. Riverside will be far more commercially focused. It's our expectation that the operational activity that is left will be complex and specialised – and that will amount to less than 100 people.

The new company will handle all the straightforward operational activity, using more automated systems and new technology. We expect that this would employ around 300 people.

[Offers an immediate chance for them to have their questions answered]
I know that for most of you, this is not a surprise and you will have many questions. You will have the opportunity to raise questions later on in the session, and I'm sure that some of your issues will be addressed by Harry, as I now hand over to him. Thank you.

Adam hands over to Harry, who takes over on centre stage:

Harry: *[Picks up immediately on a positive and reassuring point]*
Thanks Adam. Hello everyone, I'm Harry Blue, Head of HR and Communication. So as Adam said, your terms and conditions will remain the same and be protected under what are known as the TUPE legislations. Therefore as far as the initial transition, people should see no change to their contracts of employment, pension schemes or location.

When you were invited to this session, it was explained that we wouldn't have all the detail as to when areas will be affected. What we intend to ensure is that staff who transfer will not be adversely affected in terms of pension rights or entitlements or benefits, in the period following their transfer until their redundancy or redeployment. But, there may be some impact. We are looking at the detail of the impact in areas such as the Sharesave Scheme.

Get tough with heart

What we can tell you is how the company intends to ensure people are supported in a fair and consistent manner and within the spirit of the law.

Harry then goes into the detail of areas including Job Security Agreements (JSA) worked out with the recognised trade union for those employees affected by change. He talks about redeployment opportunities within Riverside and its parent company. He explains enhanced compensation and notice arrangements as well as pension benefits and redundancy. He is clear about what information he is not in a position to provide at the session:

Harry: What HR will not be providing today are estimates of redundancy packages and pension benefits that may result from the decision to sign the partnership contract with Match. We will do this soon after the contract is signed.

[Putting needs of staff first, he explains the plans to support them]
Riverside is committed to supporting staff who are faced, through no fault of their own, with having to find another job. Internal redeployment arrangements will operate but it's recognised that there may be many people in our case for whom this process will not be an option and will therefore need to search for employment outside the company.

We've put in place an outplacement support programme which will be run by Do Well plc (DW), a specialist independent external company. Outplacement refers to a career management consultancy that assists people who have experienced, or shortly will be experiencing the loss of their job. DW has been selected because it is the world's leading outplacement services organisation, with a proven record in delivering effective programmes for our new parent company.

The benefits of an Outplacement support are numerous and with DW, Riverside will tailor the outplacement service to Riverside staff needs in a fitting timetable. Here are some key benefits for you.

You will receive objective and professional support during a period of personal and professional transition which will help to restore and maintain your self confidence and morale – **you have the facility of one to one discussions with trained, independent professionals in this field.**

You will receive help to make clear decisions regarding present and future career goals – **you have access to workshops to discuss personal and career goals.**

You will be equipped with skills to evaluate career alternatives and target the most effective ways to achieve your objectives – all of which will last the whole of your working life – **you have help, support and advice to achieve new skills and focus on the right career.**

Although DW will not actually find you a job – we have asked them to provide a 'Career Centre' on site at Riverside for the relevant period. The career centre will provide resources, information, advice and support. It will give you the competitive edge over others in the same position – **you will be supplied databases with other company details and information, for those organisations looking to recruit.**

Harry then explains in detail the forthcoming HR consultation process for impacted staff – what consultation covers, when it will start, what further meetings are planned for when as well as medium-to-longer-term plans. He asks for local representatives to be nominated in the business, so they too can be involved in the consultation process. He adds:

Harry: In terms of consultation, people will be kept informed by regular briefings and team meetings, consultation briefing documents, our company newsletters and individual one-to-one consultation. As well as support from HR and DW, you will also receive help from your management team and from Miti our communication specialist whom most of you know well. We also have a reward scheme in place for your loyalty to the company through this difficult time. Kirsty will now explain.

Harry hands over to Kirsty:

Kirsty: *[Focusing immediately on what is needed and how staff will be supported]*

Thanks very much Harry. I'm Kirsty Star, Head of Customer Contact Centre. I would like to cover what the operational areas need to focus on at this challenging time, how management will support you and how the company will reward your loyalty.

What we must focus on: During this period of significant change, the operational teams need to maintain our service to our consumers and retailers (business as normal) and manage the potential transfer, work with the Transformation Team as well as manage the relationship with Match.

We understand that this will be demanding and stretching and will undoubtedly place greater stress on the people within our area.

How we will do this: We will focus on only maintaining business as normal and managing transfer activities, with no distractions from other projects. We will ensure that we have the right people in the right roles, at the right time, for the right length of time. We'll be fair and equitable to our team and we will reward loyalty.

Management support: Managers will continue to support you through this time by, maintaining an open door policy – please talk to your manager if you need to. They will also be running regular surgeries and coffee mornings and will hold effective team briefings. They are available and will be scheduling in one to one meetings with you.

Rewarding Loyalty: Our loyalty bonus scheme begins in April and rewards you for your performance, attendance and loyalty during this period.

Kirsty goes on to explain in detail the criteria for loyalty payments which are measured on performance and attendance. She finishes by adding:

Kirsty: Your local line manager will implement and monitor the loyalty bonus scheme in your area and will give you more details as it is agreed.

So as you can see, the company and operational management are committed to helping you seek alternative careers, through outplacement, assisting you through strong line management support and investing money in recognition of the work and loyalty, that I'm sure you will show.

Finally, I'd like to say a big thank you for your hard work over the last few months. I know it's a very unsettling time and I, and the rest of the management team really appreciate your commitment.

Adam and Kirsty on stage between them, set up a Q & A session:

Adam: *[Rounds up, leaving them with ten minutes to get refreshments and an immediate chance to let off steam and get questions answered]*

I'm sure you'll have many questions relating to what you have heard today. What we would like to do is give you the opportunity to discuss your issues, concerns and questions with your colleagues first.

In groups of about ten to fifteen people, please break into areas around the room or just outside in the coffee area and discuss the questions you have. Take a pad and pencil from Miti at the back and write your questions down. Nominate a speaker in your group. In ten minutes we will gather back in this room and each nominated speaker will be able to raise questions to us: Harry, Kirsty and myself.

We would like this to be a very open session – think about how this news (potential redundancies and loyalty bonus alike) makes you feel and frame your questions in that context.

See you all back here in ten minutes. Thank you.

Useful tips to help you get tough with heart

As a senior manager your role as an Innovative Communicator is a pastoral one. It's not just a clinical, abstract leadership role, it's about being there with your people in times of trouble, taking responsibility to communicate the bigger picture eyeball-to-eyeball when the news is bad.

The first crucial step is the need to show you have gone the extra mile to communicate face to face (online doesn't count). It is the direct human interaction and experience that sets the tone and the way forward. You are then in a strong position to cleverly utilise a range of channels including the social media at your disposal.

- If you have to deliver tough news, mentally put yourself in their shoes when planning – "how would I appreciate receiving this news?" Remember that if your staff do not see and feel the emotional benefits, you are operating a tick-box exercise.

- Dedicate time and energy to plan your bigger picture communication strategy so that it puts respect for your people at its heart. How can you add the personal touch? Who can you bring on board in your front-line staff? How best to communicate each stage?

- Take care of yourself if this is challenging for you. Do you need support or guidance in order to play your part effectively? Who could you ask if you needed help?

- Recognise the severity of the challenges your staff face and prepare to give them the appropriate practical support to help them (for example to find other roles or jobs).

- Make sure clear tough facts are delivered with compassion, understanding and sensitivity.

- However tough it gets, keep your staff regularly and consistently informed. Give them clarity at a time of uncertainty.

Getting tough with heart means your message is communicated clearly, accurately and honestly whether in writing or face-to-face. Your message will involve:

- **Preparation:** do your homework before a challenging meeting, talk to key individuals, assess needs and appropriate ways forward and how you can be supportive in the face of their fears.

- **Facts:** present these clearly and simply, these are the bones of your message and cannot be denied.

- **Clarity:** present a clear and simple plan, with clear reasonable choices if necessary.

- **Compassion:** put yourself in their shoes in preparation for anything you may say write or do, take care to avoid insensitivity or impersonality. Express understanding of their dilemma when with them.

- **Support:** offer the practical and human support they need to make their situation easier.

- **Integrity:** do what you say you will do, show that they can trust you to play your part.

- **Respect:** show respect for their needs and reactions, aim to act in a fair and reasonable way.

- **Conviction:** believe in your own skills, abilities and experience and promise what you know you can deliver.

- **Honesty:** come clean, call a spade a spade, tell them the truth so that what you say aligns with the experience of their reality. (This avoids rumour mills, corridor conversations, chaos and confusion). This way, they will believe in you.

- **Grace:** warmth and humility can add strength to your delivery. A sense of propriety and consideration of others will engender a spirit of goodwill.

- **Patience:** Offer them the time they deserve to process and digest difficult news, especially when it impacts their lives. Your tolerance and understanding will act as a role model for calmly enduring trying circumstances with composure and dignity.

Without the above (or a good dose of them) your communication is likely to be received as insensitive and with that comes reluctance by your people to help you achieve "operational efficiencies" or other tough goals you need to achieve.

The art of persuasion

Getting tough with heart is about warmth, not aggression or distance or coldness. It is about presenting firm, clear facts, involving people in conversation about potential options, offering support and reassurance, gaining trust and respect and doing what you say you will do with everyone's best interests at heart. Getting people on board when there is actually no choice for them involves the skill of persuasion.

We read earlier the detailed proposals presented by the three senior executives to their staff. Their "get tough with heart" presentations proved highly successful but were not arrived at easily. There was a lot of discussion, planning and preparation beforehand as their initial reaction to delivering difficult news face-to-face had been to avoid doing so. It was my job to persuade them to understand and accept the value of speaking directly to their people. This required being tough in terms of discipline, focus and achieving the right outcome for the critical task at hand.

Persuading the "get tough with heart" sceptics to push their boundaries

Miti in a room with four senior executives having called a meeting to establish a common strategy for communicating decisions about mass redundancies.

The meeting begins. There is urgency and so far no agreement.

Miti: *[With courtesy and grace]*
Gentlemen, thank you for your time. I know it's precious, so I

hope we can really make progress and agree clear actions to take matters forward. It's been great to hear your individual views of the task at hand and how you each think it should be managed. I may be wrong, so please correct me if I am. I just wondered whether you'd all managed to share your individual views and perspectives with each other?

Long momentary silence, I realise that they haven't actually talked to each other in any depth about their views and how to handle a series of unpalatable messages about large scale redundancies.

Having previously talked with each executive at length individually, I know that they fundamentally disagree on how to handle the crises. I understand how tough this is for them and why they have therefore stalled in meeting each other on this particular topic.

Miti: [Empathetically]
Well, I thought it might be a good place to start if we spent the first fifteen minutes hearing each of your perspectives and how you see the best way to deliver the news.

After fifteen minutes it's clear to each one of them that they disagree with each other on how to handle delivering bad news. What they do agree on however is that someone else (not them) will be doing it. The "someone else" though, has yet to be defined. Leaving it to their communication and HR departments had not worked well to date (I suspect due to the fact that they could not get any decisions out of the people I was now speaking to). In short their communication strategy was non-existent and urgently in need of pulling together.

Miti : [Summarising clearly to show she has understood the situation so far]
As I see it, you are making 3000 people redundant, phasing it over sixteen months, and those people need to hear that message and the plans behind it in such a way that they will still do a sterling job for the business up until the day they leave, and for some that day is still some time way off. Is this right?

Exec 1: Yes, that sum matters up.

Miti: This is a big announcement which I would suggest they need to hear from you directly in the first instance. They need to hear that it's something that while unfortunate and regrettable you are determined to see through on their behalf with support for them, and we'll need to do so with compassion and heart.

[Executives reaction: rabbit-in-headlights look but they now have something in common. They are fully present and alert, Miti has their attention]

Exec 2: Well Miti, we're not sure how that would work. If this approach is necessary, and we need to work that through, can managers or HR not take this on?

Miti: *[Presenting argument with conviction, clear facts, warmth]* Gentlemen, I promise the approach of appealing to emotion through heart and compassion at this difficult time will make all the difference. These are huge redundancies and you need staff buy-in. You currently don't have it, and you'll have even less of it if this news isn't delivered in a way that holds their attention for the right reasons. You have one shot at this. The other big piece of the jigsaw is, *[smiling supportively]*, you need to personally deliver this news at least once.

Exec 3: Is it really necessary for us to be involved at that level of detail?

Miti: *[offering a choice firmly, in which they assess the risk]* It depends what you want. If you want staff to stay on side, preserve the good will and avoid potentially grim external publicity, I would strongly recommend it. If you want to take the risk of not achieving this outcome with another option, then that's a choice open to you of course.

Exec 4: We can't afford the risk of negative publicity with disgruntled employees. It's so hard to control that with social media these days. But actually we need the good will, there's no doubt about it. Miti why is it necessary for us to be so involved?

Miti: *[Clear truths and facts but appealing to the common threads of humanity]*
The staff you are making redundant, see you as the folk who made those decisions. You're the executive, they hold you responsible. They want to hear the news from you, and see whether they matter given all the years' service and commitment many of them have given to your business. In short they are human and they want to be treated as such. Being made redundant is painful. If you have no visibility in the process of handling this difficult time, it sends a simple message to them that you don't care, and the consequences of that is grave for your business.

Execs: *[Silence]*

Exec 2: We'd just be making fools of ourselves . . . .

Miti: *[Picking up his dis-ease and offering empathy and support, showing what responsibility she will take and making reassuring promises]*
We'll work as a team, and my role is to help you with this. I will be supporting you and making it as easy as possible for you all the way. I'll develop a full communication strategy, which will include a communication plan for all your individual sites and locations impacted, pull in a range of people and develop their skills too. I'll pull a plan together for your talks and speeches and we can run through them and practice as much as you want well before D-day. There'll be structure, focus and clarity of messages underpinned by your visible support, understanding and heart in the delivery of those messages. Gentlemen it's going to be fine.

[Executive reaction: Shoulders, beginning to relax, smiles beginning to appear, feeling relieved that there is warmth, understanding and support for their task]

Exec 3: Well, I think given the choices we face, we have to go for the one that ensures we get it right. It's useful to find out in this room that we actually hadn't agreed on much prior to this meeting.

Get tough with heart

Exec 1: The matter is urgent and we want to avoid a fall out. I agree, we go with Miti's plan. What to you think?

Execs: Yes we're in. We'll go with it. So Miti you're going to sort out next steps?

Miti: *[Reinforcing confidence, taking responsibility, showing efficiency, working supportively with them to enable them to feel she has their best interests at heart]*
Yes, having talked to all of you at length, and now we've agreed to go with delivering the news personally in the first instance, I'll develop, plan and write a full communications strategy and deliver that in the next fortnight. I've already spoken to most people I need to round the business, so the communication plan will incorporate and integrate the needs of the business as a whole. We can then really hit the ground running action-wise. Should I arrange another meeting with your PAs in a week? I have to confess I was hoping for this outcome, so I've actually written the bulk of a communications strategy for you. I'll just need to develop your part in the visible commitment of senior management. I can have that ready as a full draft communication strategy for you within the week. So our next meeting could be next week.

Exec 1: Do it. Sounds like a plan.

Exec 3: Yes, I have to say I feel better about this.
[Executive 2 and 4 nodding in agreement]

Exec 1: Thanks Miti, Look forward to next week.

Miti: You're most welcome.

From the receiving end

The following is an extract from a contribution to the company newsletter from one of the impacted employees in the case study we read earlier in the chapter. It is a genuine document, though I have changed the name and date to respect confidentiality.

> *I'm Lily White and I'm a member of the back office support team. I started my role as an Innovative Communicator (IC) on the staff representative board (SRB) on 15 March 2010 and work closely with senior management on behalf and in the interests of staff who are impacted by the forthcoming job losses in the Central Division. I think the Innovative Communicator and SRB roles have worked really well in bringing concerns, issues and needs of colleagues to the direct attention of senior management. We regularly meet with Terry Smith our Executive Sponsor and give him plenty of direct feedback from staff.*
>
> *A highlight for me was last year when having given Terry some robust feedback, he organised an all day event for staff to express and address issues and concerns. The feedback received both on the day and post event is that my colleagues were very happy with the discussions and outcomes. A lot of issues were resolved and they were left feeling motivated. On a personal note, I feel genuinely proud to have had a part in this. It is great to see the whole staff representative process and have it proved that it did and still does work. Looking at the bigger picture, I understand why the company is making these job changes. It is regrettably necessary to make some big changes in order to survive. I fully understand what this means to some staff, as my husband is one of those affected and will lose his job as a result of the job cuts. But I believe we will be a stronger business following the transformation.*

Imagine the impact and influence, this article from "one of their own" made on both staff staying in the business and staff exiting the business. The visible commitment of senior management, delivered ambassadors for the business, which in turn delivered wider buy-in. The innovative role played by communication was key to delivering this success.

Getting tough with heart – summary

> Communicate your message clearly, accurately, honestly with integrity and empathy.
>
> Provide clarity at a time of uncertainty (say what is and is not, what you do know and do not).
>
> Put yourself in their shoes and understand how tough a situation it is for others.
>
> The tougher your message, the greater the need to communicate you also care about their plight.
>
> Getting people on board where there is actually no choice for them involves the skill of persuasion.
>
> Back up your communication of support with action that delivers this to provide emotional benefits (otherwise all you are offering is warm meaningless platitudes).

Questions to think about

- Think of a time when you coped when you had to get tough. Run the story in detail in your mind. What happened? How well did you cope?

- How did you rate your ability to put "heart" at the centre of the tough situation in terms of the way you communicated?

- Is there a situation you are likely to encounter where you might benefit from using the "tough with heart" skills?

- Which of the "tough with heart skills" do you do well or not so well? Discuss this with a friend or colleague.

Exercise

If you do one thing today, pick three things from this chapter that made a particular impression on you, and find a way to use them as a communication approach, in your next tough situation or encounter at work.

8

Have a life to bring to the table

> *"A joyful state is a basic human need, so a healthy dollop of fun and smiles in the workplace will help create a priceless business."*
> **Miti Ampoma**

On 19 April 2012, on television, *Sky News* reported that the British supermarket giant Tesco, "wants to put the love back in its business". This news followed Tesco's announcement that it had seen the worst trading performance in decades in its UK business, an announcement which wiped off a fifth of the company's value in a single day.

The drop in fortune made big news, but what was equally fascinating was the language used by the media to describe Tesco's plans to reverse its fortunes, the most fascinating being the word "love". Tesco and love . . . love and Tesco . . . . The point that came across was that Tesco wanted people to associate the company with *feelings* and *emotion* and that this was central in their plans to turn their UK business round.

No more cogs in wheels

What I've consistently found is that the bigger the business the higher the likelihood that the heart and soul of the organisation is squeezed and sacrificed at the expense of bureaucracy and profits. Many employees (and customers) in turn feel they are treated as commodities, statistics, "just another number" or as one employee expressed "I'm a meaningless cog in the wheel instead of a human being whose needs are being met". This is the recurring perception or sentiment of many, imagined or real.

A fifty to sixty hour week in the workplace, which many staff do in large organisations does not allow for a healthy balanced life. Just think, if you are tired, stressed and fed up because most of your life is taken up by the hours at work, are you inclined to want to really engage or talk to anyone or would you prefer to get your head down and have a relationship with your computer screen where you don't have to speak at all?

Most people (as employees or customers) want to be associated with an organisation where there is "life", where people smile, a fun presence, some *joie de vivre!* Emotions are the language that connect the body and mind. That language is translated by and in the way we communicate with each other. The way each of us feels in the work place therefore makes a huge difference to how we communicate, and how we communicate with each other drives performance.

> **Feeling emotionally well, uplifts our mood, it is good for the soul, and it is good for us, as we work together and with each other. If there is genuine, appropriate joie de vivre in the workplace, we want to stay or be associated with it. Organisations ignore this fact in practice, at their peril.**

It is perfectly possible to have an organisation which is a fun place to work and which also makes substantive profit (which is what great businesses are there to do). The two are not mutually exclusive. You can have both.

> **It is when a human being has time for a life (outside the workplace) that they are at their most powerful to be innovative, clear thinking and can fully contribute fresh original ideas in the workplace.**

To be an Innovative Communicator and perform at your best at work, you need to have a life and it is really important to make the time for one. When you have a full life, you are a better communicator, because you feel well. It is a simple but crucial equation of cause and effect.

Make time for the fun to happen

I love travel, I love spas and I am always up for a health-based holiday. I have an elderly parent who lives abroad whom I need to see and am

Have a life to bring to the table

committed to. I also love Christmas in the sun. (It is important to stress that these are my particular passions that work for me. We all have different hobbies and interests that are right for us, as you will too.) So, here's what I do. I book my travel trips by the end of April each year – that is two weeks in the summer. One of those weeks is abroad while the second week is at a favourite health club in the UK. My further two weeks covers Christmas and New Year and I'll opt for sunnier climes like Bali or Barbados. Once I have booked my passions and priorities in the diary and parted with money to secure that time for myself, I have made a commitment to give value and time to my life. It makes me feel better instantly knowing I have those passions to look forward to and through them, I am fully replenished and in a position to give value and time to others in both my workplace and in other relationships. Communication is at the centre of those relationships and has to land well. It lands well, because I feel great!

If your thing is golf, danger sports, or racing, make sure you make it happen. Book it in the diary so you have something to look forward to.

Note: My holidays are built into the calendar, managed and shared so as to avoid being away from work when it is absolutely imperative that I am there.

Make time for your hobbies, interests and relationships – professional and personal – and you are likely to be a much better communicator at work. Interests and hobbies shared with work colleagues are fabulous for building work relationships. It opens up conversations, provides potential common ground and strengthens bonds. In other words, it is a powerful communication tool.

Of course it is a juggling act but that is part of the fun in life where we aim to juggle our various balls successfully, so to speak. When we do that well – and like most things that comes with practice – we feel great.

However it's about more than just having a life outside the workplace, it's about being able to share your experiences appropriately, sharing something valuable of who you are as a person to enable the building of rapport, good will, common ground and trust between you and your colleagues. This is one of the hallmarks of the Innovative Communicator.

Sharing of this kind needs to be seen as a strength rather than a loss of face or over-familiarity.

Life's joy in spontaneity

Picture this. One Thursday morning I was sitting working, beavering away at my computer, when Sue, a work colleague, happened to mention that she was trying to sell two tickets rather unsuccessfully on eBay. Having asked what tickets, she replied they were tickets to see the veteran singer George Michael. My heart did a double flip. I love George Michael! I said I was in, I'd have them. She hesitatingly added that the concert wasn't actually in London. "Where then?" I asked? "It's actually in Paris," she replied. The main reason Sue was having problems selling the tickets on eBay was of course that someone would need to part with their money and pay online and then travel to Paris (with the cost that would incur) to meet a total stranger to collect the tickets. In the era of distrust we live in, one can understand why the take-up for these genuine tickets wasn't of "must do" proportions. So Sue still had these tickets. They were also VIP tickets so the seats were likely to be vintage. Intuitively, I knew this was an opportunity too good to miss. I decided mentally there and then I was going to go, if at all possible.

This was Thursday, the concert was in Paris the following Tuesday. I just needed to make it happen, because all said and done, I could see myself at that George Michael concert. As I was cooing and aahing with verbal enthusiasm at the mere but imaginatively detailed thoughts of singing along to George Michael lyrics in Paris, another colleague sitting near me was listening and watching me intently.

Within two hours I had checked diaries and schedules, confident that it was do-able, arranged to take the afternoon off the following Tuesday, and I'd bought the concert ticket from Sue. I was buzzing with excitement and couldn't stop smiling, quietly dancing at intervals in my chair.

The colleague who had been watching me make my arrangements then said to me: "So you're going to Paris then to see George Michael". I replied, "Yes I am. Bring it on" and I started humming a soulful George Michael tune. She smiled and started humming with me and replied in between our jointly hummed chorus "I love George Michael". Bopping up and down in my chair in syncopation to the rhythm of our George Michael song, I added "Well there's a spare ticket going. Why don't you come? It'll only mean an afternoon off, and we'll be back in the office the next morning". By this time I had my hands in the air as I hit a George Michael high note. "That's it. I'm coming", said my colleague. We went to find Sue with the hallowed eBay ticket and Bob's your uncle, both tickets were sold.

We got permission to have a half day off for the following Tuesday. I stress that even though the decision was made spontaneously, we took care to ensure that it was possible, feasible and acceptable with regard to work responsibilities. At lunch-time, we booked our travel on Euro star to Paris, and by the end of our lunch break we had two seats on the Eurostar and hotel accommodation booked for an overnight stay in Paris. The two of us would join Sue and her friend in Paris for the concert. We were going to Paris to rock with George! How fabulous was that as a treat to look forward to?

The concert itself the following Tuesday, as a George Michael fan was of course absolutely amazing. The seats were VIP and we were six rows from the front. The atmosphere was electric with anticipation and excitement and I can tell you George truly delivered. One knew one was seeing a great artist of our time perform live and it was incredible. Though this was in October, it happened to be one of those very late Indian summer weeks in Europe and that particular week in October was the new hot summer. So walking with work colleagues on a very warm Indian summer evening in Paris to the Bercy Stadium, being part of a truly great event, and walking back together to our hotel in the warm late evening Parisian breeze, building relationships so organically and naturally, was a memorable experience. We barely had five hours sleep as we were back to the train station in the morning at 6.00am to catch the Eurostar back to London for me to make the 9.00am Programme Management team meeting. And we did. It was such fun! Everyone in the office wanted to know what it was like. Again as a talking point it was great for building relations around who we were as people, adding another layer in the development of building strong relationships. Needless to say I also built excellent relationships with the work colleagues I shared the experience with.

A few weeks after returning from Paris, George Michael was to cancel the rest of his world tour as he sadly fell seriously ill. As he rarely tours now, it turned out that those of us who saw him that evening at the Bercy Stadium in Paris in October 2011, were one of the last privileged to do so for a very long while. How fortunate do I feel to have made the decision to go to that concert, seize the opportunity and make it happen? Very fortunate indeed.

Useful tips to help you "bring your life to the table"

Be well mentally, physically and spiritually and you will touch others' lives with your smile, your presence, your genuineness.

- **Stay physically fit and well:** Eat as healthily as you can, exercise regularly and make it fun. No point dragging yourself to the gym to suffer if the gym is not your thing. If you don't like it, the lack of motivation and dislike will translate into your professional and personal life. Instead, exercise in a way you love, be it dancing, walking, gardening, golf or any other physical activity you actually enjoy. Make it fun not torture.

- **Stay mentally fit and well:** Mental stimulation and peace of mind are critical to success. Success is communicated. Have hobbies and interests you enjoy that stimulate your mind.

- **Stay spiritually fit and well:** Regardless of your religious preferences (or not), it is healthy to feel spiritually well in the sense that your own soul knows a peace, a sense of joy, a cup is half full rather than half empty attitude to life. Whatever way in which you achieve this is an individual choice, but the feeling that all is well in yourself – despite the challenges life can throw at us – is a path well striving for.

- **Interests, hobbies, passions:** Commit time to your interests, hobbies and passions. Book them in the diary, part with money to ensure they happen if appropriate. Don't just dream about them. Do them. Enjoy them and share that enjoyment.

- **Create a support network:** When you have a life to bring to the table you are in a position to create a personal support network that works for you, so you can be fully present and focused in the workplace. Your support network is likely to include a close circle of people you know, love and trust who are with you through thick and thin, through the tough as well as the good times. They love you and keep you balanced and grounded too.

- **Have downtime:** Make time for yourself by building in personal downtime where you can relax and just be. Refrain from doing! Though energising and fun, being an Innovative Communicator is hard work. It is important to create a balance between empowering others in the work place and carving time for your own valuable downtime in which you recharge and renew.

- **Treat yourself:** Invest in you by treating yourself with the kindness and generosity you would treat others. Spend a proportion of your income on activities that enhance your well being, quality of life and makes you look and feel great. It could be from buying fresh flowers, to buying sports gear, clothes that flatter to taking a decent holiday. These are just examples of self-investment. You know what floats your boat, keeps you feeling in top shape, so you are in a position to give your best as an Innovative Communicator.

- **Be open to possibilities:** Say yes more often than no. If you are open to possibilities and you are up for what life has to offer in experience, the creation of opportunities will come your way. The more experience in your life the stronger a communicator you become.

As an Innovative Communicator you can pass on your skills and benefits to your people and business. You are also a role model for spontaneity and *joie de vivre* in the workplace, which frees up stuck attitudes that block communication and flexibility.

- **Be wise with time:** With twenty-four hours a day as the great leveller, we all have the same amount of it. Use your time to make daily choices that really make a difference to the quality of your life. In the workplace, this approach helps you, your colleagues and business to achieve your goals.

- **Make every day count:** Aim to make every day memorable. Of course there is a place for planning the future and reflecting on the past and learning from it, but both these activities are there to inform, enrich and aid the present. So it is worth making every day count.

- **Enjoy life, have fun:** Love what you do and how you do it. Stay positive, look on the bright side of life and you will attract like-minded people around you. You will also inject a vitality and energy in the workplace. As an Innovative Communicator you will challenge where necessary, but will do this in a way that leaves people smiling, feeling better and getting the best from you. People will want to work with or for you. You continue to surprise. You are a joyful soul.

- **Give generously:** Be generous in spirit. Pass on your skills and knowledge. As an Innovative Communicator, share and exchange ideas. It is emotionally beneficial for you to give and for others to receive your expertise.

Let your enthusiasm be contagious

The emotional benefits of self-care will give you the competitive edge as an Innovative Communicator. You will generate care, excitement, sizzle and positive emotional benefits in others. You will touch others with your smile, your presence and authenticity.

When we feel in top form, we communicate with imagination, depth and empathy and this is vital in the fast paced modern workplace. If this talk of joy, soul, life and smiles leaves any reader uncomfortable or sceptical, it is worth remembering that our supermarket giant Tesco, an undisputed bell weather for the state of British business and the economy, wants to put the love back into its business, as a central plank of its strategy to turn its spiralling fortunes round.

Who wouldn't want to make time for life?

An Innovative Communicator makes time to have a healthy and full life that brings them joy outside work. Their joy as human beings, transfers to their character, personality and behaviour in the workplace. This creates a healthy holistic balance in who they are and the contribution they make.

Have a life to bring to the table – summary

> Make time for things you love doing, do them and share your experiences.
>
> Seize an opportunity to develop relationships at work through shared interests outside work.
>
> Appreciate and value communication that is uplifting and fun, rather than complaining about everything.
>
> Life's joy is in being spontaneous sometimes.
>
> Be the catalyst for infectious enthusiasm.
>
> Be generous in spirit. It lands well and motivates others.

Questions to think about

- Where are you on the scale of one to ten with a healthy work/life balance? (One is poor, ten is excellent.)

- What floats your boat outside work? What are your passions, hobbies and interests? How can you build these into your schedule?

- How can you find ways of sharing your "life" to enable better relationships at work? Do you feel comfortable doing this?

- In what way are you committing to your health and well-being?

- If you are not looking after your general well-being, what small first step would you enjoy taking towards this goal?

Exercise

If you do one thing today, identify a hobby, interest, passion or activity as part of your life outside work, which if shared could enhance what happens at work.

9

Keep sparkling

> *"We can only benefit from feeling bright and sparkly in the workplace. Having some sparkle in our being makes us feel alive and well. It's good for our soul and good for business. It's worth incorporating into business goals and worth striving for. The vehicle for this, is innovative communication."*
>
> **Miti Ampoma**

What makes people sparkle or fizzle out!

The following is genuine feedback that I received from an employee who I will call Quentin. The FTSE 100 company he worked for had been through major organisational change of its people, systems and processes.

> **Quentin – team member**
>
> *"I work in a very large company and I was one of the front-line staff at the receiving end of a big re-organisation. A lot of my colleagues lost their jobs as a result of the changes. I was a "survivor" but the whole journey of 18 months was traumatic at times to be honest. For many of us, what made the biggest difference was the way the company handled the communication of the changes and what was going on for us.*

At first it was awful, big fanfare announcing changes, promises, then nothing for months. Everyone was in the dark, no one seemed to care or tell us what was going to happen.

Anyway, after ten months it all changed. They brought in new people and suddenly we had a lot of information, discussions, people we needed to speak to visiting us regularly in our local offices. We got to know them, they got to know us and we felt we could ask questions and get quick responses. We could see they really cared about communicating with us and we felt they had our interests at heart even though it was an awful situation. It sounds so simple but it made such a difference. Many of my friends who were obviously upset to be losing their jobs, were pleased to be treated so well and with respect, that they would work for the company again given the chance. They worked their socks off till their last day, because they were kept in the picture so well. We were shown respect and felt valued because the management were on the spot and there for us. What was great was it wasn't a one-week wonder. It was consistent and regular and it made us feel we mattered and someone cared about us. Why couldn't they have taken this approach in the first place?"

Staff feedback about the way the changes were handled

The following comments are genuine and were sent in by staff who worked for several blue chip companies that had been through major organisational change.

"Thank you for the honest, straight-forward relevant communication. Truly heroic."

"The communication has been very informative, clear, concise and warm, if that's the right expression! It's made a big difference to our people."

"The enthusiasm and passion for simple and honest communication methods have been great for staff. More please."

"I am sad to be leaving, but if I have to be made redundant the way I have been treated and communicated with is the best I could ever hope for. Thank you."

"What a breath of fresh air to have jargon free communication that makes sense."

"Great to find out more about our future. Clear message of the way forward."

"Presentations have been very interesting, easy to understand, informative and well presented. Good use of people i.e. range of people, styles of communication and tasks. Never boring!"

Paul was Quentin's director and these were his views at the end of the transformation programme he led.

> **Paul – Director**
>
> *"It has been an astonishing journey. I've been a director of these kind of large organisational change programmes in business for thirty years and I have to admit I had no idea this kind of communication could be so powerful and effective.*
>
> *I was reluctant to embrace this 'innovative communication' approach, because that's not the way we normally operate. But there's no question it's played a significant role in our business success, no doubt at all. Getting people bought in and emotionally on side, makes for a successful business but it's actually very hard to achieve and I can see it's a skill. It can only be achieved with this level and type of communication.*
>
> *For us, our changes and job losses were extensive and while we announced people were going to lose their jobs we weren't letting them leave for another twelve to eighteen months. It meant we needed them here on the one hand, but had given them the boot on the other. In the interim period, it would be fair to say that they did the business proud in their unwavering commitment and professionalism. The bottom line is all our performance indicators,*

> such as staff turning up to work remained unaffected throughout. And in their feedback and surveys, staff consistently told us communication played a key role in how they felt and therefore responded.
>
> As senior management our relationship with managers, team leaders and front line staff has changed beyond recognition largely due to the relationship building and managing people on site and not just from a distance. We've gained much "national benefit" from local understanding, engagement and regular meaningful interaction. This creative, inclusive and collaborative approach has reaped huge rewards for the business. So I'm won over.
>
> **There are two lessons for me as a Director. We need to operate our communications differently from now on and clearly more 'innovatively' than we have done in the past! We need to incorporate a lot more creative approaches like Team Talk and Face2face into our communication recognising the need to put people at the centre of our delivery strategies. We need to make that really happen and not just say we will. So yes, I'm sold".**

The lessons learned from feedback like this is that if you communicate innovatively, your people will perform at their best and keep sparkling.

Having core values and beliefs

I am passionate about passing on as much of my business communication experience as possible, so that the best of human relationships can and will transform businesses for the greater good. We all have an Innovative Communicator in us! This focus keeps me motivated.

Over the years, I have personally tried to keep sparkling as much as possible in how I work in business communication. As a human being, I don't always hit the mark. Some days are less sparkling than others. There have been days in the midst of tough change and chaos that I've marked for the uphill folder! However, every day, I strive to live and align my personal philosophy, values and beliefs with my profession.

What helps me to keep sparkling are my profound beliefs in the following key things:

- Everyone needs compassion and deserves to be heard.
- Everyone wants to feel valued and they can be.
- Communicating with integrity and humanity are paramount.
- Offering and receiving trust and loyalty are paramount.
- I commit to walking my talk.
- I get a buzz from being authentic – being who I really am.
- There is always a way forward – how can I best communicate it?
- The cup is half full, rather than half empty – how can I inspire people to see it?
- Anything can be changed for the better.
- "If not me then who, if not now then when?" – *Hillel the Elder*.
- Sharing the knowledge gets people on side and avoids rumours.
- "Life shrinks and expands in proportion to one's courage" – *Anais Nin*.
- Aim for perfection and settle for excellence.
- I take pride in how far I have come and have faith in how far I can go.
- It feels good to smile warmly and keep a sense of humour, especially when the going gets tough! In the greater scheme of things it'll be fine – I strive to attune to the bigger picture, to the power of being positive.
- Happy staff, happy customers, more profits and successful business are dependent on there being a heart, a soul and a humanity in the organisation.

Tips to help you keep sparkling

I invite you to look again and take ownership of the key messages in each chapter in the way that is most appropriate for you, mindful of where you are in your own communication journey. Going through the summaries, questions and exercises will help you evaluate how good you are within each chapter subject. Then it's about setting yourself a manageable goal in the areas you find challenging.

Once you start taking action in bite-size chunks or as is appropriate for you, observe the effect your innovative communication skills have on

Keep sparkling

your people, observing simply what happens when they feel valued, observing what works, what creates bonds, loyalty and respect. Practice, practice, practice is the key. Keep consciously making the effort to practice your communication skills and eventually it will become a habit.

It is a well-known scientific fact that habits are formed by repetition and practice. Becoming an Innovative Communicator is no different. It's like learning to ride a bike or drive a car. You learn, adopt and practice the skills. Eventually you are able to do it automatically. Through practice, a strong brain pathway is uploaded and operates seamlessly in your mind. In short, new behaviours create new thought patterns which eventually become habit and the normal way to do things.

We can all learn to become skilled Innovative Communicators. We can look for ways small and large, to put people back at the centre of our businesses. When we see it working, in small ways, we feel confident in committing the time and energy to larger issues. Every large business communication issue is a collection of smaller ones and little good ones add up!

In the words of Dr Andrew Curran, consultant neurologist and author of *The Little Book of Big Stuff about the Brain*: "Our job in life is to remove the barriers in our lives without distortion so we can shine to our optimum. The key to everything is emotional connection". Dr Curran's view is equally applicable in business.

Key points to remember along the way

If you have felt inspired by things you have read in this book, you will be making changes in some of the ways you communicate with your people. I've summarised from each chapter some key points to keep in mind.

Chapter 1: Meet the Innovative Communicator

The persona of the Innovative Communicator is not a position or a job description. Nor is it a role you can or should pass on to your public relations, communication or HR department (though of course the

The Innovative Communicator

people in these areas may already have or might also wish to enhance their skills as Innovative Communicators).

The Innovative Communicator is a way of behaving, a way of treating people; a do-as-you-would-be-done-by-philosophy that respects people's need to be recognised, whilst not being afraid to get tough if necessary. Anyone including you can be an Innovative Communicator, and it applies to any relationship you form. In being one in the work place, you will play a significant role in driving business performance and profits. Communicating with "soul" will feel good the more you do it, the more you respect and empower your people.

Qualities: *Optimistic, appropriate enthusiasm, can-do attitude, insightful, disciplined, flexible, works well as part of a team, operates well under pressure, respectful while knowing the boundaries, fair, creative.*

Chapter 2: Build deep relationships

There will be opportunities for building new and deep relationships every day. It requires the skills of connecting people to one another and you will find yourself noticing the development of your ability to enable genuine communication powered from the heart, enabling soul, humanity, integrity and loyalty to be at the centre of your business. You build relationships through communicating face-to-face, voice-to-voice contact, getting to know your key people as individuals, valuing them for their skills and enabling them to know you and your values too. When the Innovative Communicator builds deep relationships, the result is emotional benefit for people associated with the business. You will notice how the sparkle builds up.

Qualities: *People matter, caring, a sharer, a thinker, intuitive, emotional maturity and intelligence, able to articulate the concern for wellbeing of staff while also articulating the needs of the business, approachable, speaks to the best in people, listener, trusted confidante.*

Chapter 3: Get your team on board

Getting your team on board is about creating and maintaining team spirit at its peak. The Innovative Communicator is a catalyst for enabling abundant team spirit and for getting people enthusiastic and bought in for what needs doing. You're about influencing team members that goals are worth striving for and encouraging them to see the value in participating. You continuously need to persuade your team that you are all in it together, and keep them on side. You'll be looking for opportunities to get people together where the quality of communication, whether it be problem solving or fun, is admirable.

Qualities: Positive energy, sociable, articulate, ability to calm and soothe egos, ability to motivate, ability to explain strategies clearly, humour, warmth.

Chapter 4: Build your strategy

An Innovative Communicator develops, builds and operates a communication strategy that is relevant and action driven. You need to "get stuff done". Whether your task is a simple project or wide-ranging and all encompassing, your communication plan will operate a robust disciplined framework that allows for flexibility to think on one's feet and act quickly and consistently to deliver the most effective solutions. It will take people's needs into consideration, particularly when grim news has to be delivered.

Qualities: Clarity, ability to feel and communicate conviction, a doer, makes people feel included, flexible, thinks outside the box, practical, values the way in which strategies are communicated to people.

Chapter 5: Push your own boundaries

As an Innovative Communicator you become familiar with pushing your own boundaries, stretching yourself and being comfortable with being uncomfortable. You'll be looking for opportunities to get involved in activities or situations that will ensure you stay in touch with grassroots, reality (the way most people are) and humanity. You see the value in strengthening your inner resources, so you can go beyond your normal stretch to create an empowering internal environment in which people and the business thrive.

Qualities: Curious, tenacity, focussed, determined, values personal growth, willing to learn from mistakes and try something new, personal vulnerability, honesty, deep breath and action!

Chapter 6: Step forward with courage

As you face tough situations, your ability to communicate effectively is of critical importance. Stepping forward with courage is about what you are able to do inside your head to think clearly, keep perspective, bear with fortitude and take appropriate action, when you are in the eye of the storm, when chaos reigns or the chips are down. You will be challenged to feel your own courage, keep your sense of control, calm and clarity within the maelstrom so that you effectively communicate your way through chaos. Be bold, be clear, and remember we all deserve to be treated with humanity.

Qualities: *Brave, feel the fear and do it anyway, do what is right and good, be willing to put yourself on the line in the interests of the greater good, perseverance, no quitter!*

Chapter 7: Get tough with heart

You will undoubtedly be challenged to make tough decisions and the Innovative Communicator is no pushover. Getting tough with heart requires the discernment of 'facing the music', knowing when and where to draw the line and exercising the art of persuasion. It's not what you say, it's the way you say it. This is about getting people to do what they need or have to do when there is little choice. It's about turning the unwelcome into as palatable and acceptable as possible, so the initially reluctant can become part of the solution (rather than the problem), despite often Herculean hurdles. The Innovative Communicator will strive to shape-shift and change the status quo for the greater good.

Qualities: *Ability to persuade, ability to stand firm with clear reasoning, influence, secure and engage the commitment of others, committed to supporting people adversely affected, resourceful, quick to grasp complex information, make sense of it, give it clarity and make it accessible and simple for others to understand, values the way information is put across.*

Chapter 8: Have a life to bring to the table

As an Innovative Communicator you will have personal interests and hobbies outside work, which inform who you are as a person and by extension influence your approach to communication in the work place. You bring something enriching of yourself and of your life to your work. You inject a healthy dose of joie de vivre, smiles and fun back into your business environment. People gravitate towards you for your positive energy and you set an example to those around you.

Qualities: *Looks on the bright side of life, enthusiasm, smiles, generosity of spirit, personality combination of project manager disciplines, flexibility and spontaneity for life.*

Chapter 9: Keep sparkling

The development and nurturing of these attributes and qualities, keeps the Innovative Communicator sparkling!

> *Miranda, my local flower stall business owner continues to keep sparkling as an Innovative Communicator. She is a symbol of a business with innovative communication at its heart, delivering happy staff, happy customers and sustainable, well-deserved profits. She warms the cockles of many hearts! She provides emotional benefit in bucket loads.*

What Miranda does, every business or organisation no matter its size – through you – can achieve the same. I invite you to join the Innovative Communicator's club.

Let's raise a toast to Innovative Communicators everywhere!

Next steps

If you've enjoyed this book, I'd like to help you apply what we've covered to your own business.

I've created a free video series for you, as well as a weekly newsletter, which will help you put the soul back into your business.

Join a growing community of employees, team managers and CEOs who are committed to happy staff, happy customers and more profits! Simply scan this QR code:

or enter http://miticom.co.uk/freeupdates into your browser and you'll be taken to a place where you can sign up. Once you've done this, I'll send you the video series and we can stay in touch as you position yourself as the Innovative Communicator within your business.

I look forward to connecting with you personally.

Best wishes

Miti

About the author

Miti Ampoma is an award-winning business communication specialist with over fifteen years' experience, leading change and transformation communication programmes in FTSE 100 companies, financial services and corporate institutions. Her skills and expertise are highly sought after, particularly on merger and acquisitions, joint ventures, shared services, business process re-engineering and large scale, complex integration programmes. She is a Fellow of the Chartered Institute of Public Relations. She has a previous career as a television news journalist and documentary producer-director.